Big Data Fundamentals

Dr. Elangovan G.
Assistant Professor
Department of Data Science and Business Systems,
SRM Institute of Science and Technology,
SRM Nagar,
Kattankulathur.

Dr. N. Susitha
Associate Professor
Dept. of Computer Science,
School of Arts and Science,
Vinayaka Mission's Research Foundation (DU),
Chennai.

Dr. S. Kavitha
HoD / Associate Professor
Dept. of Computer Science,
School of Arts and Science,
Vinayaka Mission's Research Foundation (DU),
Chennai.

978-1-312-75952-7

© All Right Reserved by the Publisher.

First Edition: March – 2023

Lulu Publisher

This book has been published with all reasonable efforts taken to make the material error-free after the consent of the author. No part of this book shall be used, reproduced in any manner whatsoever without written permission from the author, except in the case of brief quotations embodied in critical articles and reviews.

The Author of this book is solely responsible and liable for its content including but not limited to the views, representations, descriptions, statements, information, opinions and references. The Content of this book shall not constitute or be construed or deemed to reflect the opinion or expression of the Publisher or Editor. Neither the Publisher nor Editor endorse or approve the Content of this book or guarantee the reliability, accuracy or completeness of the Content published herein and do not make any representations or warranties of any kind, express or implied, including but not limited to the implied warranties of merchantability, fitness for a particular purpose. The Publisher and Editor shall not be liable whatsoever for any errors, omissions, whether such errors or omissions result from negligence, accident, or any other cause or claims for loss or damages of any kind, including without limitation, indirect or consequential loss or damage arising out of use, inability to use, or about the reliability, accuracy or sufficiency of the information contained in this book.

ISBN: 978-1-312-75952-7

AUTHOR PROFILE

Dr. G. Elangovan has completed his Ph.D. in Information and Communication Engineering from Anna University, Chennai and is currently working as an Assistant Professor in the Department of Data Science and Business Systems at SRM Institute of Science and Technology, Kattankulathur. He has completed his M.E degree in Computer Science and Engineering from Bannari Amman Institute of Technology, Anna University and B.E degree in Computer Science and Engineering under Anna University, Chennai. He has more than 10 years of teaching and research experience and has several research publications in reputed International Journals/Conferences. His research area includes Graph based Data Analytics, Theoretical Computer Science and Machine learning.

Dr. N. Susitha holds Master of Computer Applications from Alagappa Chettiar College of Engineering and Technology, Karaikudi in 2004, Master of Philosophy in Computer Science from Bharathidasan University, Trichirappalli in 2012. She qualified SET in 2018 and was conferred Doctorate from Mother Teresa Women's University, Kodaikanal in 2020. She worked as Programmer Analyst in Cognizant Technology Solutions, Chennai. Having 11 years teaching experience and currently working as Associate Professor in Department of Computer Science, School of Arts and Science, Vinayaka Mission's Research Foundation (Deemed to be University), Chennai. Her research interest includes Biometrics, Digital Image Processing and Machine Learning. She has published 11 reputed International Journals.

 **Dr. S. Kavitha** is currently working as a HOD & Associate professor in Department of Computer Science, School of Arts and Science, AVIT Campus-Chennai – 603104 TamilNadu, India since 2006.She has around 16 years of Experience in teaching both UG and PG Computer Science Students. She Received her Ph.D Degree in computer Science from Vinayaka Mission's Research Foundation, Salem and obtained her Master of Computer Applications Degree from Mother Teresa Women's University, kodaikanal. Dr.S.kavitha is an expertise in Programming Languages like C,C++ and Java and also keen interest on Advanced Technologies like Artificial Intelligence, Data Science and Big Data.

Contents

Chapter I

Understanding Big Data

1.1 Concepts and Terminology	3
1.2 Big Data Characteristics	13
1.3 Different Types of Data	18

Chapter II

Business Motivations and Drivers for Big Data Adoption

2.1 Marketplace Dynamics	25
2.2 Business Architecture	27
2.3 Business Process Management	31
2.4 Information and Communications Technology	32
2.5 Internet of Everything (IoE)	38

Chapter III

Big Data Adoption and Planning Considerations

3.1 Organization Prerequisites	42
3.2 Data Procurement	43
3.3 Privacy	43
3.4 Security	44
3.5 Provenance	45
3.6 Limited Realtime Support	46
3.7 Distinct Performance Challenges	47
3.8 Distinct Governance Requirements	47
3.9 Distinct Methodology	48
3.10 Clouds	49

3.11 Big Data Analytics Lifecycle	49

Chapter IV

Enterprise Technologies and Big Data Business Intelligence

4.1 Online Transaction Processing (OLTP)	73
4.2 Online Analytical Processing (OLAP)	73
4.3 Extract Transform Load (ETL)	74
4.4 Data Warehouses	75
4.5 Data Marts	76
4.6 Traditional BIE	76
4.7 Big Data BIE	79

Chapter V

Big Data Storage Concepts

5.1 Clusters	85
5.2 File Systems and Distributed File Systems	85
5.3 NoSQL	87
5.4 Sharding	87
5.5 Replication	89
5.6 Sharding and Replication	95
5.7 CAP Theorem	99
5.8 ACID	102
5.9 BASE	106

Chapter VI

Big Data Processing Concepts

6.1 Parallel Data Processing	112
6.2 Distributed Data Processing	112
6.3 Hadoop	113

6.4 Processing Workloads	114
6.5 Cluster	116
6.6 Processing in Batch Mode	117
6.7 Processing in Realtime Mode	132

Preface

Drawing on case studies like Amazon, Facebook, the FIFA World Cup and the Aadhaar scheme, this book looks at how Big Data is changing the way we behave, consume and respond to situations in the digital age. It looks at how Big Data has the potential to transform disaster management and healthcare, as well as prove to be authoritarian and exploitative in the wrong hands.

The latest offering from the authors of Artificial Intelligence: Evolution, Ethics and Public Policy, this accessibly written volume is essential for the researcher in science and technology studies, media and culture studies, public policy and digital humanities, as well as being a beacon for the general reader to make sense of the digital age.

Authors

Chapter I

Understanding Big Data

Big Data is a field dedicated to the analysis, processing, and storage of large collections of data that frequently originate from disparate sources. Big Data solutions and practices are typically required when traditional data analysis, processing and storage technologies and techniques are insufficient. Specifically, Big Data addresses distinct requirements, such as the combining of multiple unrelated datasets, processing of large amounts of unstructured data and harvesting of hidden information in a time-sensitive manner.

Although Big Data may appear as a new discipline, it has been developing for years. The management and analysis of large datasets has been a long-standing problem—from labor-intensive approaches of early census efforts to the actuarial science behind the calculations of insurance premiums. Big Data science has evolved from these roots.

In addition to traditional analytic approaches based on statistics, Big Data adds newer techniques that leverage computational resources and approaches to execute analytic algorithms. This shift is important as datasets continue to become larger, more diverse, more complex and streaming-centric. While statistical approaches have been used to approximate measures of a population via sampling since Biblical times, advances in computational science have allowed the processing of entire datasets, making such sampling unnecessary.

The analysis of Big Data datasets is an interdisciplinary endeavor that blends mathematics, statistics, computer science and subject matter expertise. This mixture of skillsets and perspectives has led to some confusion as to what comprises the field of Big Data and its analysis, for the response one receives will be dependent upon the perspective of whoever is answering the question. The boundaries of what constitutes a Big Data problem are also changing due to the ever-shifting and advancing landscape of software and hardware technology. This is due to the fact that the definition of Big Data takes into account the impact of the data's characteristics on the design of the solution environment itself. Thirty years ago, one gigabyte of data could amount to a Big Data problem and require special purpose computing resources. Now, gigabytes of data are commonplace and can be easily transmitted, processed and stored on consumer-oriented devices.

Data within Big Data environments generally accumulates from being amassed within the enterprise via applications, sensors and external sources. Data processed by a Big Data solution can be used by enterprise applications directly or can be fed into a data warehouse to enrich existing data there. The results obtained through the processing of Big Data can lead to a wide range of insights and benefits, such as:

- Operational Optimization
- Actionable Intelligence
- Identification of New Markets
- Accurate Predictions
- Fault and Fraud Detection
- More Detailed Records
- Improved Decision-Making
- Scientific Discoveries

Evidently, the applications and potential benefits of Big Data are broad. However, there are numerous issues that need to be considered when adopting Big Data analytics approaches. These issues need to be understood and weighed against anticipated benefits so that informed decisions and plans can be produced.

1.1 Concepts and Terminology

As a starting point, several fundamental concepts and terms need to be defined and understood.

Datasets

Collections or groups of related data are generally referred to as datasets. Each group or dataset member (datum) shares the same set of attributes or properties as others in the same dataset. Some examples of datasets are:

- Tweets stored in a flat file
- A collection of image files in a directory
- An extract of rows from a database table stored in a csv formatted file
- Historical weather observations that are stored as xml files

Figure 1.1 shows three datasets based on three different data formats.

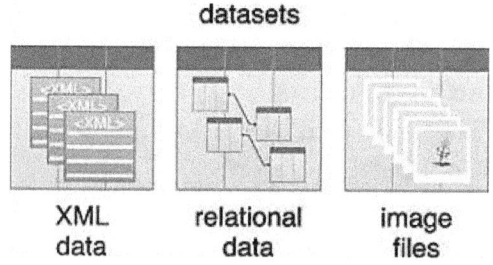

Figure 1.1 Datasets can be found in many different formats.

Data Analysis

Data analysis is the process of examining data to find facts, relationships, patterns, insights and/or trends. The overall goal of data analysis is to support better decision-making. A simple data analysis example is the analysis of ice cream sales data in order to determine how the number of ice cream cones sold is related to the daily temperature. The results of such an analysis would support decisions related to how much ice cream a store should order in relation to weather forecast information. Carrying out data analysis helps establish patterns and relationships among the data being analyzed. Figure 1.2 shows the symbol used to represent data analysis.

Figure 1.2 The symbol used to represent data analysis.

Data Analytics

Data analytics is a broader term that encompasses data analysis. Data analytics is a discipline that includes the management of the complete data lifecycle, which encompasses collecting, cleansing, organizing, storing, analyzing and governing data. The term includes the development of analysis methods, scientific techniques and automated tools. In Big Data environments, data analytics has developed methods that allow data analysis to occur through the use of highly scalable distributed technologies and frameworks that are capable of analyzing large volumes of data from different sources. Figure 1.3 shows the symbol used to represent analytics.

Figure 1.3 The symbol used to represent data analytics.

The Big Data analytics lifecycle generally involves identifying, procuring, preparing and analyzing large amounts of raw, unstructured data to extract meaningful information that can serve as an input for identifying patterns, enriching existing enterprise data and performing large-scale searches.

Different kinds of organizations use data analytics tools and techniques in different ways.

Take, for example, these three sectors:

- In business-oriented environments, data analytics results can lower operational costs and facilitate strategic decision-making.
- In the scientific domain, data analytics can help identify the cause of a phenomenon to improve the accuracy of predictions.
- In service-based environments like public sector organizations, data analytics can help strengthen the focus on delivering high-quality services by driving down costs.

Data analytics enable data-driven decision-making with scientific backing so that decisions can be based on factual data and not simply on past experience or intuition alone.

There are four general categories of analytics that are distinguished by the results they produce:

- Descriptive analytics
- Diagnostic analytics
- Predictive analytics
- Prescriptive analytics

The different analytics types leverage different techniques and analysis algorithms. This implies that there may be varying data, storage and processing requirements to facilitate the delivery of multiple types of analytic results. Figure 1.4 depicts the reality that the generation of high value analytic results increases the complexity and cost of the analytic environment.

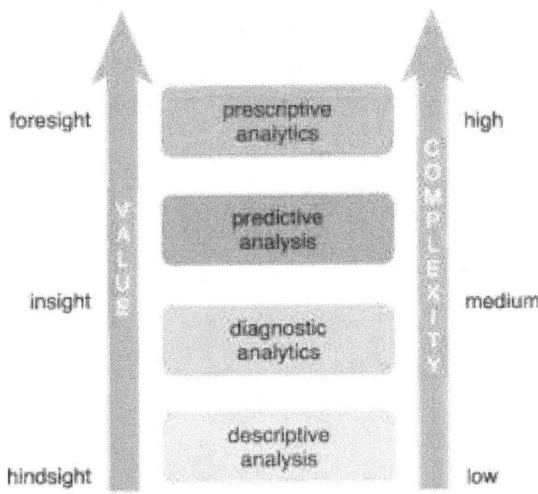

Figure 1.4 Value and complexity increase from descriptive to prescriptive analytics.

Descriptive Analytics

Descriptive analytics are carried out to answer questions about events that have already occurred. This form of analytics contextualizes data to generate information.

Sample questions can include:

- What was the sales volume over the past 12 months?
- What is the number of support calls received as categorized by severity and geographic location?
- What is the monthly commission earned by each sales agent?

It is estimated that 80% of generated analytics results are descriptive in nature. Value-wise, descriptive analytics provide the least worth and require a relatively basic skillset.

Descriptive analytics are often carried out via ad-hoc reporting or dashboards, as shown in Figure 1.5. The reports are generally static in nature and display historical data that is presented in the form of data grids or charts. Queries are executed on operational data stores from within an enterprise, for example a Customer Relationship Management system (CRM) or Enterprise Resource Planning (ERP) system.

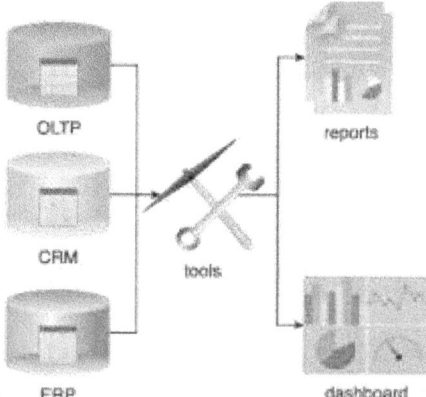

Figure 1.5 The operational systems, pictured left, are queried via descriptive analytics tools to generate reports or dashboards, pictured right.

Diagnostic Analytics

Diagnostic analytics aim to determine the cause of a phenomenon that occurred in the past using questions that focus on the reason behind the event. The goal of this type of analytics is to determine what information is related to the phenomenon in order to enable answering questions that seek to determine why something has occurred.

Such questions include:

- Why were Q2 sales less than Q1 sales?
- Why have there been more support calls originating from the Eastern region than from the Western region?
- Why was there an increase in patient re-admission rates over the past three months?

Diagnostic analytics provide more value than descriptive analytics but require a more advanced skillset. Diagnostic analytics usually require collecting data from multiple sources and storing it in a structure that lends itself to performing drill-down and roll-up analysis, as shown in Figure 1.6. Diagnostic analytics results are viewed via interactive visualization tools that enable users to identify trends and patterns. The executed queries are more complex compared to those of descriptive analytics and are performed on multi-dimensional data held in analytic processing systems.

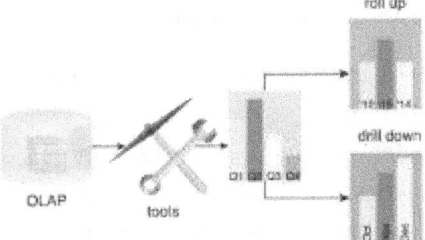

Figure 1.6 Diagnostic analytics can result in data that is suitable for performing drill-down and roll-up analysis.

Predictive Analytics

Predictive analytics are carried out in an attempt to determine the outcome of an event that might occur in the future. With predictive analytics, information is enhanced with meaning to generate knowledge that conveys how that information is related. The strength and magnitude of the associations form the basis of models that are used to generate future predictions based upon past events. It is important to understand that the models used for predictive analytics have implicit dependencies on the conditions under which the past events occurred. If these underlying conditions change, then the models that make predictions need to be updated.

Questions are usually formulated using a what-if rationale, such as the following:

- What are the chances that a customer will default on a loan if they have missed a monthly payment?
- What will be the patient survival rate if Drug B is administered instead of Drug A?
- If a customer has purchased Products A and B, what are the chances that they will also purchase Product C?

Predictive analytics try to predict the outcomes of events, and predictions are made based on patterns, trends and exceptions found in historical and current data. This can lead to the identification of both risks and opportunities.

This kind of analytics involves the use of large datasets comprised of internal and external data and various data analysis techniques. It provides greater value and requires a more advanced skillset than both descriptive and diagnostic analytics. The tools used generally abstract underlying statistical intricacies by providing user-friendly front-end interfaces, as shown in Figure 1.7.

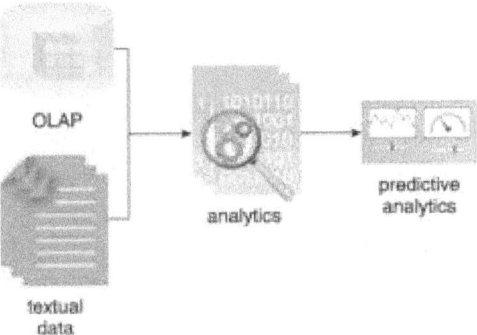

Figure 1.7 Predictive analytics tools can provide user-friendly front-end interfaces.

Prescriptive Analytics

Prescriptive analytics build upon the results of predictive analytics by prescribing actions that should be taken. The focus is not only on which prescribed option is best to follow, but why. In other words, prescriptive analytics provide results that can be reasoned about because they embed elements of situational understanding. Thus, this kind of analytics can be used to gain an advantage or mitigate a risk.

Sample questions may include:

- Among three drugs, which one provides the best results?
- When is the best time to trade a particular stock?

Prescriptive analytics provide more value than any other type of analytics and correspondingly require the most advanced skillset, as well as specialized software and tools. Various outcomes are calculated, and the best course of action for each outcome is suggested. The approach shifts from explanatory to advisory and can include the simulation of various scenarios.

This sort of analytics incorporates internal data with external data. Internal data might include current and historical sales data, customer information, product data and business rules. External data may include social media data, weather forecasts and government-produced demographic data. Prescriptive analytics involve the use of business rules and large amounts of internal and external data to simulate outcomes and prescribe the best course of action, as shown in Figure 1.8.

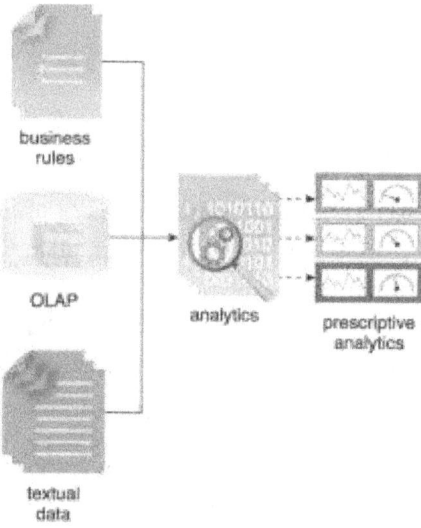

Figure 1.8 Prescriptive analytics involves the use of business rules and internal and/or external data to perform an in-depth analysis.

Business Intelligence (BI)

BI enables an organization to gain insight into the performance of an enterprise by analyzing data generated by its business processes and information systems. The results of the analysis can be used by management to steer the business in an effort to correct detected issues or otherwise enhance organizational performance. BI applies analytics to large amounts of data across the enterprise, which has typically been consolidated into an enterprise data warehouse to run analytical queries. As shown in Figure 1.9, the output of BI can be surfaced to a dashboard that allows managers to access and analyze the results and potentially refine the analytic queries to further explore the data.

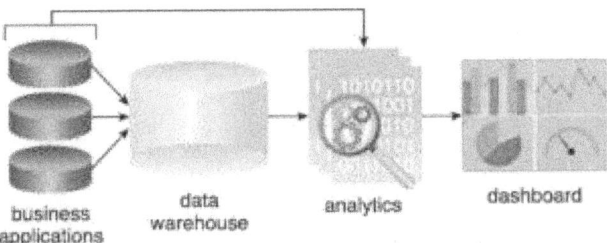

Figure 1.9 BI can be used to improve business applications, consolidate data in data warehouses and analyze queries via a dashboard.

Key Performance Indicators (KPI)

A KPI is a metric that can be used to gauge success within a particular business context. KPIs are linked with an enterprise's overall strategic goals and objectives. They are often used to identify business performance problems and demonstrate regulatory compliance. KPIs therefore act as quantifiable reference points for measuring a specific aspect of a business' overall performance. KPIs are often displayed via a KPI dashboard, as shown in Figure 1.10. The dashboard consolidates the display of multiple KPIs and compares the actual measurements with threshold values that define the acceptable value range of the KPI.

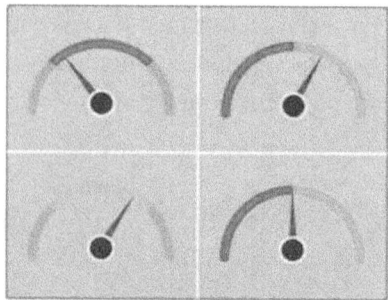

KPI dashboard

Figure 1.10 A KPI dashboard acts as a central reference point for gauging business performance.

1.2 Big Data Characteristics

For a dataset to be considered Big Data, it must possess one or more characteristics that require accommodation in the solution design and architecture of the analytic environment. Most of these data characteristics were initially identified by Doug Laney in early 2001 when he published an article describing the impact of the volume, velocity and variety of e-commerce data on enterprise data warehouses. To this list, veracity has been added to account for the lower signal-to-noise ratio of unstructured data as compared to structured data sources. Ultimately, the goal is to conduct analysis of the data in such a manner that high-quality results are delivered in a timely manner, which provides optimal value to the enterprise.

This section explores the five Big Data characteristics that can be used to help differentiate data categorized as "Big" from other forms of data. The five Big Data traits shown in Figure 1.11 are commonly referred to as the Five Vs:

- volume
- velocity
- variety
- veracity

- value

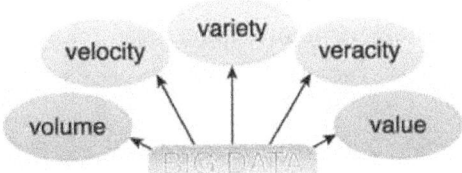

Figure 1.11 The Five Vs of Big Data.

Volume

The anticipated volume of data that is processed by Big Data solutions is substantial and ever-growing. High data volumes impose distinct data storage and processing demands, as well as additional data preparation, curation and management processes. Figure 1.12 provides a visual representation of the large volume of data being created daily by organizations and users world-wide.

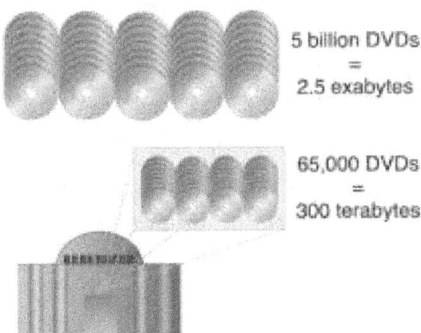

Figure 1.12 Organizations and users world-wide create over 2.5 EBs of data a day. As a point of comparison, the Library of Congress currently holds more than 300 TBs of data.

Typical data sources that are responsible for generating high data volumes can include:

- Online transactions, such as point-of-sale and banking

- scientific and research experiments, such as the large hadron collider and atacama large millimeter/submillimeter array telescope
- sensors, such as gps sensors, rfids, smart meters and telematics
- social media, such as facebook and twitter

Velocity

In Big Data environments, data can arrive at fast speeds, and enormous datasets can accumulate within very short periods of time. From an enterprise's point of view, the velocity of data translates into the amount of time it takes for the data to be processed once it enters the enterprise's perimeter. Coping with the fast inflow of data requires the enterprise to design highly elastic and available data processing solutions and corresponding data storage capabilities.

Depending on the data source, velocity may not always be high. For example, MRI scan images are not generated as frequently as log entries from a high-traffic webserver. As illustrated in Figure 1.13, data velocity is put into perspective when considering that the following data volume can easily be generated in a given minute: 350,000 tweets, 300 hours of video footage uploaded to YouTube, 171 million emails and 330 GBs of sensor data from a jet engine.

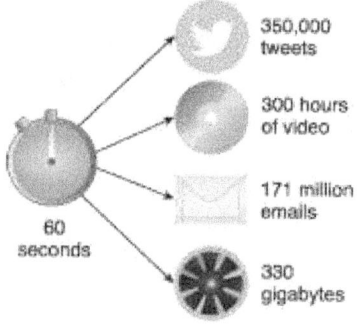

Figure 1.13 Examples of high-velocity Big Data datasets produced every minute include tweets, video, emails and GBs generated from a jet engine.

Variety

Data variety refers to the multiple formats and types of data that need to be supported by Big Data solutions. Data variety brings challenges for enterprises in terms of data integration, transformation, processing, and storage. Figure 1.14 provides a visual representation of data variety, which includes structured data in the form of financial transactions, semi-structured data in the form of emails and unstructured data in the form of images.

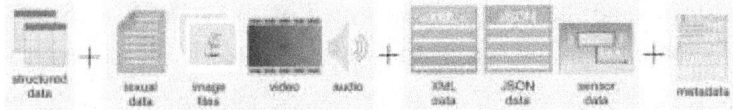

Figure 1.14 Examples of high-variety Big Data datasets include structured, textual, image, video, audio, XML, JSON, sensor data and metadata.

Veracity

Veracity refers to the quality or fidelity of data. Data that enters Big Data environments needs to be assessed for quality, which can lead to data processing activities to resolve invalid data and remove noise. In relation to veracity, data can be part of the signal or noise of a dataset. Noise is data that cannot be converted into information and thus has no value, whereas signals have value and lead to meaningful information. Data with a high signal-to-noise ratio has more veracity than data with a lower ratio. Data that is acquired in a controlled manner, for example via online customer registrations, usually contains less noise than data acquired via uncontrolled sources, such as blog postings. Thus the signal-to-noise ratio of data is dependent upon the source of the data and its type.

Value

Value is defined as the usefulness of data for an enterprise. The value characteristic is intuitively related to the veracity characteristic in that the higher the data fidelity, the more value it holds for the business. Value is also dependent on how long data processing takes because analytics results have a shelf-life; for example, a 20 minute delayed stock quote has little to no value for making a trade compared to a quote that is 20 milliseconds old. As demonstrated, value and time are inversely related. The longer it takes for data to be turned into meaningful information, the less value it has for a business. Stale results inhibit the quality and speed of informed decision-making. Figure 1.15 provides two illustrations of how value is impacted by the veracity of data and the timeliness of generated analytic results.

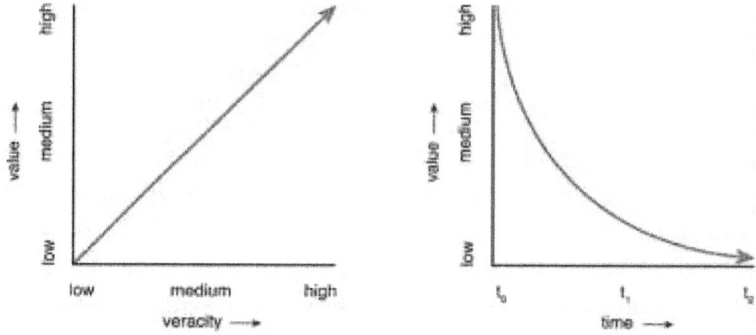

Figure 1.15 Data that has high veracity and can be analyzed quickly has more value to a business.

1.3 Different Types of Data

The data processed by Big Data solutions can be human-generated or machine-generated, although it is ultimately the responsibility of machines to generate the analytic results. Human-generated data is the result of human interaction with systems, such as online services and digital devices. Figure 1.16 shows examples of human-generated data.

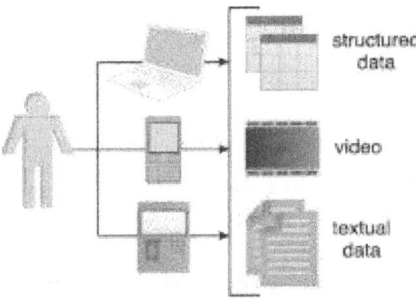

Figure 1.16 Examples of human-generated data include social media, blog posts, emails, photo sharing and messaging.

Machine-generated data is generated by software programs and hardware devices in response to real-world events. For example, a log file captures an authorization decision made by a security service, and a point-of-sale system generates a transaction against inventory to reflect items purchased by a customer. From a hardware perspective, an example of machine-generated data would be information conveyed from the numerous sensors in a cellphone that may be reporting information, including position and cell tower signal strength. Figure 1.17 provides a visual representation of different types of machine-generated data.

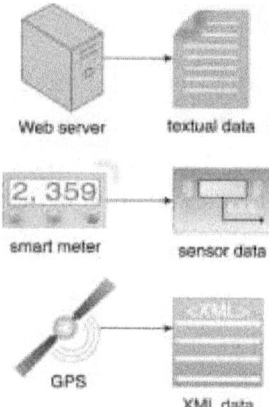

Figure 1.17 Examples of machine-generated data include web logs, sensor data, telemetry data, smart meter data and appliance usage data.

As demonstrated, human-generated and machine-generated data can come from a variety of sources and be represented in various formats or types. This section examines the variety of data types that are processed by Big Data solutions. The primary types of data are:

- Structured data
- Unstructured data
- Semi-structured data

These data types refer to the internal organization of data and are sometimes called data formats. Apart from these three fundamental data types, another important type of data in Big Data environments is metadata. Each will be explored in turn.

Structured Data

Structured data conforms to a data model or schema and is often stored in tabular form. It is used to capture relationships between different entities and is therefore most often stored in a relational database. Structured data is frequently generated by enterprise applications and information systems like ERP and CRM systems. Due to the abundance of tools and databases that natively support structured data, it rarely requires special consideration in regards to processing or storage. Examples of this type of data include banking transactions, invoices, and customer records. Figure 1.18 shows the symbol used to represent structured data.

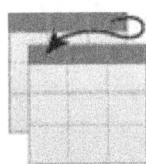

Figure 1.18 The symbol used to represent structured data stored in a tabular form.

Unstructured Data

Data that does not conform to a data model or data schema is known as unstructured data. It is estimated that unstructured data makes up 80% of the data within any given enterprise. Unstructured data has a faster growth rate than structured data. Figure 1.19 illustrates some common types of unstructured data. This form of data is either textual or binary and often conveyed via files that are self-contained and non-relational. A text file may contain the contents of various tweets or blog postings. Binary files are often media files that contain image, audio or video data. Technically, both text and binary files have a structure defined by the file format itself, but this aspect is disregarded, and the notion of being unstructured is in relation to the format of the data contained in the file itself.

video   image files   audio

Figure 1.19 Video, image and audio files are all types of unstructured data.

Special purpose logic is usually required to process and store unstructured data. For example, to play a video file, it is essential that the correct codec (coder-decoder) is available. Unstructured data cannot be directly processed or queried using SQL. If it is required to be stored within a relational database, it is stored in a table as a Binary Large Object (BLOB). Alternatively, a Not-only SQL (NoSQL) database is a non-relational database that can be used to store unstructured data alongside structured data.

Semi-structured Data

Semi-structured data has a defined level of structure and consistency, but is not relational in nature. Instead, semi-structured data is hierarchical or graph-based. This kind of data is commonly stored in files that contain text. For instance, Figure 1.20 shows that XML and JSON files are common forms of semi-structured data. Due to the textual nature of this data and its conformance to some level of structure, it is more easily processed than unstructured data.

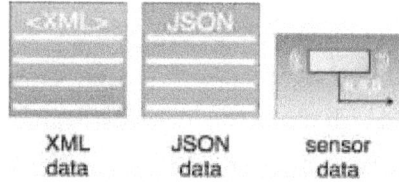

Figure 1.20 XML, JSON and sensor data are semi-structured.

Examples of common sources of semi-structured data include electronic data interchange (EDI) files, spreadsheets, RSS feeds and sensor data. Semi-structured data often has special pre-processing and storage requirements, especially if the underlying format is not text-based. An example of pre-processing of semi-structured data would be the validation of an XML file to ensure that it conformed to its schema definition.

Metadata

Metadata provides information about a dataset's characteristics and structure. This type of data is mostly machine-generated and can be appended to data. The tracking of metadata is crucial to Big Data processing, storage and analysis because it provides information about the pedigree of the data and its provenance during processing. Examples of metadata include:

- Xml tags providing the author and creation date of a document
- Attributes providing the file size and resolution of a digital photograph

Big Data solutions rely on metadata, particularly when processing semi-structured and unstructured data. Figure 1.21 shows the symbol used to represent metadata.

Figure 1.21 The symbol used to represent metadata.

Chapter II

Business Motivations and Drivers for Big Data Adoption

In many organizations it is now acceptable for a business to be architected in much the same way as its technology. This shift in perspective is reflected in the expanding domain of enterprise architecture, which used to be closely aligned with technology architecture but now includes business architecture as well. Although businesses still view themselves from a mechanistic system's point of view, with command and control being passed from executives to managers to front-line employees, feedback loops based upon linked and aligned measurements are providing greater insight into the effectiveness of management decision-making.

This cycle from decision to action to measurement and assessment of results creates opportunities for businesses to optimize their operations continuously. In fact, the mechanistic management view is being supplanted by one that is more organic and that drives the business based upon its ability to convert data into knowledge and insight. One problem with this perspective is that, traditionally, businesses were driven almost exclusively by internal data held in their information systems. However, companies are

learning that this is not sufficient in order to execute their business models in a marketplace that more resembles an ecological system. As such, organizations need to consume data from the outside to sense directly the factors that influence their profitability. The use of such external data most often results in "Big Data" datasets.

This chapter explores the business motivations and drivers behind the adoption of Big Data solutions and technologies. The adoption of Big Data represents the confluence of several forces to include: marketplace dynamics, an appreciation and formalism of Business Architecture (BA), the realization that a business' ability to deliver value is directly tied to Business Process Management (BPM), innovation in Information and Communications Technology (ICT) and finally the Internet of Everything (IoE). Each of these topics will be explored in turn.

2.1 Marketplace Dynamics

There has been a fundamental shift in the way businesses view themselves and the marketplace. In the past 15 years, two large stock market corrections have taken place— the first was the dot-com bubble burst in 2000, and the second was the global recession that began in 2008. In each case, businesses entrenched and worked to improve their efficiency and effectiveness to stabilize their profitability by reducing costs. This of course is normal. When customers are scarce, cost-cutting often ensues to maintain the corporate bottom line. In this environment, companies conduct transformation projects to improve their corporate processes to achieve savings.

As the global economies began to emerge from recession, companies began to focus outward, looking to find new customers and keep existing customers from defecting to marketplace competitors. This was accomplished by offering new products and services and delivering increased value propositions to customers. It is a very different market cycle to the one that focuses on cost-cutting, for it is not about transformation but instead innovation. Innovation brings hope to a company that it will find new ways to achieve a competitive advantage in the marketplace and a consequent increase in top line revenue.

The global economy can experience periods of uncertainty due to various factors. We generally accept that the economies of the major developed countries in the world are now inextricably intertwined; in other words, they form a system of systems. Likewise, the world's businesses are shifting their perspective about their identity and independence as they recognize that they are also intertwined in intricate product and service networks.

For this reason, companies need to expand their Business Intelligence activities beyond retrospective reflection on internal information extracted from their corporate information systems. They need to open themselves to external data sources as a means of sensing the marketplace and their position within it. Recognizing that external data brings additional context to their internal data allows a corporation to move up the analytic value chain from hindsight to insight with greater ease. With appropriate tooling, which often supports sophisticated simulation capabilities, a company can develop analytic results that provide foresight. In this case, the tooling assists in bridging the gap between knowledge and wisdom as well as provides advisory analytic results. This is the power of Big Data— enriching corporate perspective beyond introspection, from which a business can only infer information about marketplace sentiment, to sensing the marketplace itself.

The transition from hindsight to foresight can be understood through the lens of the DIKW pyramid depicted in Figure 2.1. Note that in this figure, at the top of the triangle, wisdom is shown as an outline to indicate that it exists but is not typically generated via ICT systems. Instead, knowledge workers provide the insight and experience to frame the available knowledge so that it can be integrated to form wisdom. Wisdom generation by technological means quickly devolves into a philosophical discussion that is not within the scope of this book. Within business environments, technology is used to support knowledge management, and personnel are responsible for applying their competency and wisdom to act accordingly.

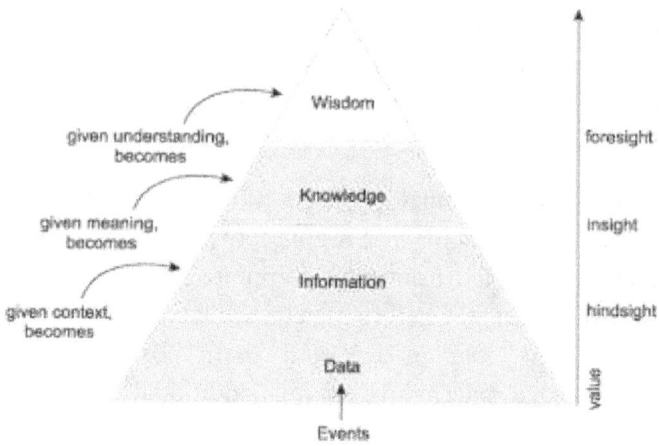

Figure 2.1 The DIKW pyramid shows how data can be enriched with context to create information, information can be supplied with meaning to create knowledge and knowledge can be integrated to form wisdom.

2.2 Business Architecture

Within the past decade, there has been a realization that too often a corporation's enterprise architecture is simply a myopic view of its technology architecture. In an effort to wrest power from the stronghold of IT, business architecture has emerged as a complementary discipline. In the future, the goal is that enterprise architecture will present a balanced view between business and technology architectures. Business architecture provides a means of blueprinting or concretely expressing the design of the business. A business architecture helps an organization align its strategic vision with its underlying execution, whether they be technical resources or human capital. Thus, a business architecture includes linkages from abstract concepts like business mission, vision, strategy and goals to more concrete ones like business services, organizational structure, key performance indicators and application services.

These linkages are important because they provide guidance as to how to align the business and its information technology. It is an accepted view that a business operates as a layered system—the top layer is the strategic layer occupied by C-level executives and advisory groups; the middle layer is the tactical or managerial layer that seeks to steer the organization in alignment with the strategy; and the bottom layer is the operations layer where a business executes its core processes and delivers value to its customers. These three layers often exhibit a degree of independence from one another, but each layer's goals and objectives are influenced by and often defined by the layer above, in other words top-down. From a monitoring perspective, communication flows upstream, or bottom-up via the collection of metrics. Business activity monitoring at the operations layer generates Performance Indicators (PIs) and metrics, for both services and processes. They are aggregated to create Key Performance Indicators (KPIs) used at the tactical layer. These KPIs can be aligned with Critical Success Factors (CSFs) at the strategic layer, which in turn help measure progress being made toward the achievement of strategic goals and objectives.

Big Data has ties to business architecture at each of the organizational layers, as depicted in Figure 2.2. Big Data enhances value as it provides additional context through the integration of external perspectives to help convert data into information and provide meaning to generate knowledge from information. For instance, at the operational level, metrics are generated that simply report on what is happening in the business. In essence, we are converting data through business concepts and context to generate information. At the managerial level, this information can be examined through the lens of corporate performance to answer questions regarding how the business is performing. In other words, give meaning to the information. This information may be further enriched to answer questions regarding why the business is performing at the level it is. When armed with this knowledge, the strategic layer can provide further insight to help answer questions of which strategy needs to change or be adopted in order to correct or enhance the performance.

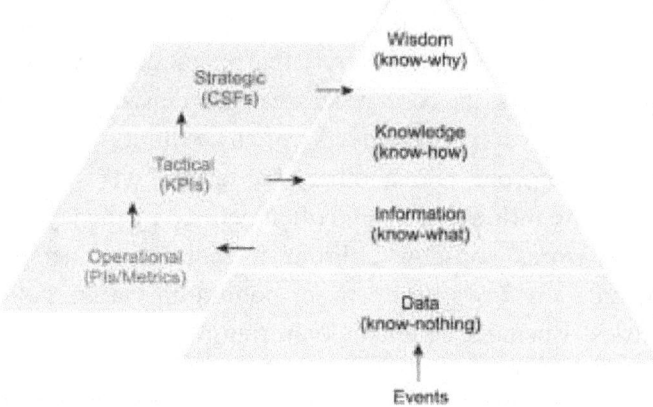

Figure 2.2 The DIKW pyramid illustrates alignment with Strategic, Tactical and Operational corporate levels.

As with any layered system, the layers do not all change at the same speed. In the case of a business enterprise, the strategic layer is the slowest moving layer, and the operational layer is the fastest moving layer. The slower moving layers provide stability and direction to the faster moving layers. In traditional organizational hierarchies, the management layer is responsible for directing the operational layer in alignment with the strategy created by the executive team. Because of this variation in regard to speed of change, it is possible to envision the three layers as being responsible for strategy execution, business execution and process execution respectively. Each of these layers relies upon different metrics and measures, presented through different visualization and reporting functions. For example, the strategy layer may rely upon balanced scorecards, the management layer upon an interactive visualization of KPIs and corporate performance and the operational layer on visualizations of executing business processes and their statuses.

Figure 2.3, a variant of a diagram produced by Joe Gollner in his blog post "The Anatomy of Knowledge," shows how an organization can relate and align its organizational layers by creating a virtuous cycle via a feedback loop. On the right side of the figure, the strategic layer drives response via the application of judgment by making decisions regarding corporate strategy, policy, goals and objectives that are communicated as constraints to the tactical layer. The tactical layer in turn leverages this knowledge to generate priorities and actions that conform to corporate direction. These actions adjust the execution of business at the operational layer. This in turn should generate measureable change in the experience of internal stakeholders and external customers as they deliver and consume business services. This change, or result, should surface and be visible in the data in the form of changed PIs that are then aggregated into KPIs. Recall that KPIs are metrics that can be associated with critical success factors that inform the executive team as to whether or not their strategies are working. Over time, the strategic and management layers injection of judgment and action into the loop will serve to refine the delivery of business services.

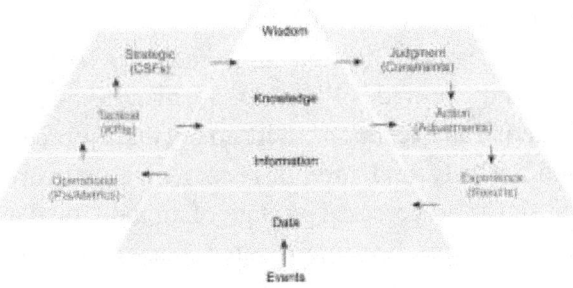

Figure 2.3 The creation of a virtuous cycle to align an organization across layers via a feedback loop

2.3 Business Process Management

Businesses deliver value to customers and other stakeholders via the execution of their business processes. A business process is a description of how work is performed in an organization. It describes all work-related activities and their relationships, aligned with the organizational actors and resources responsible for conducting them. The relationships between activities may be temporal; for example, activity A is executed before activity B. The relationships can also describe whether the execution of activities is conditional, based upon the outputs or conditions generated by other activities or by sensing events generated outside of the business process itself.

Business process management applies process excellence techniques to improve corporate execution. Business Process Management Systems (BPMS) provide software developers a model driven platform that is becoming the Business Application Development Environment (BADE) of choice. A business application needs to: mediate between humans and other technology-hosted resources, execute in alignment with corporate policies and ensure the fair distribution of work to employees. As a BADE, models of a business process are joined with: models of organizational roles and structure, business entities and their relationships, business rules and the user-interface. The development environment integrates these models together to create a business application that manages screenflow and workflow and provides workload management. This is accomplished in an execution environment that enforces corporate policy and security and provides state management for long-running business processes. The state of an individual process, or all processes, can be interrogated via Business Activity Monitoring (BAM) and visualized.

When BPM is combined with BPMSs that are intelligent, processes can be executed in a goal-driven manner. Goals are connected to process fragments that are dynamically chosen and assembled at run-time in alignment with the evaluation of the goals. When the combination of Big Data analytic results and goal-driven behavior are used together, process execution can become adaptive to the marketplace and responsive to environmental conditions. As a simple example, a customer contact process has process fragments that enable communication with customers via a voice call, email, text message and traditional postal mail. In the beginning, the choice of these contact methods is unweighted, and they are chosen at random. However, behind-the-scenes analysis is being done to measure the effectiveness of the contact method via statistical analysis of customer responsiveness.

The results of this analysis are tied to a goal responsible for selecting the contact method, and when a clear preference is determined, the weighting is changed to favor the contact method that achieves the best response. A more detailed analysis could leverage customer clustering, which would assign individual customers to groups where one of the cluster dimensions is the contact method. In this case, customers can be contacted with even greater refinement, which provides a pathway to one-to-one targeted marketing.

2.4 Information and Communications Technology

This section examines the following ICT developments that have accelerated the pace of

Big Data adoption in businesses:

- Data analytics and data science
- Digitization
- Affordable technology and commodity hardware
- Social media

- Hyper-connected communities and devices
- Cloud computing

Data Analytics and Data Science

Enterprises are collecting, procuring, storing, curating and processing increasing quantities of data. This is occurring in an effort to find new insights that can drive more efficient and effective operations, provide management the ability to steer the business proactively and allow the C-suite to better formulate and assess their strategic initiatives. Ultimately, enterprises are looking for new ways to gain a competitive edge. Thus the need for techniques and technologies that can extract meaningful information and insights has increased. Computational approaches, statistical techniques and data warehousing have advanced to the point where they have merged, each bringing their specific techniques and tools that allow the performance of Big Data analysis. The maturity of these fields of practice inspired and enabled much of the core functionality expected from contemporary Big Data solutions, environments and platforms.

Digitization

For many businesses, digital mediums have replaced physical mediums as the de facto communications and delivery mechanism. The use of digital artifacts saves both time and cost as distribution is supported by the vast pre-existing infrastructure of the Internet. As consumers connect to a business through their interaction with these digital substitutes, it leads to an opportunity to collect further "secondary" data; for example, requesting a customer to provide feedback, complete a survey, or simply providing a hook to display a relevant advertisement and tracking its click-through rate. Collecting secondary data can be important for businesses because mining this data can allow for customized marketing, automated recommendations and the development of optimized product features. Figure 2.4 provides a visual representation of examples of digitization.

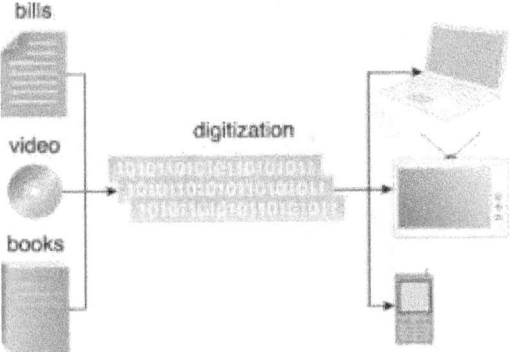

Figure 2.4 Examples of digitization include online banking, on-demand television and streaming video.

Affordable Technology and Commodity Hardware

Technology capable of storing and processing large quantities of diverse data has become increasingly affordable. Additionally, Big Data solutions often leverage open-source software that executes on commodity hardware, further reducing costs. The combination of commodity hardware and open source software has virtually eliminated the advantage that large enterprises used to hold by being able to outspend their smaller competitors due to the larger size of their IT budgets. Technology no longer delivers competitive advantage. Instead, it simply becomes the platform upon which the business executes. From a business standpoint, utilization of affordable technology and commodity hardware to generate analytic results that can further optimize the execution of its business processes is the path to competitive advantage.

The use of commodity hardware makes the adoption of Big Data solutions accessible to businesses without large capital investments. Figure 2.5 provides an example of the price decline associated with data storage prices over the past 20 years.

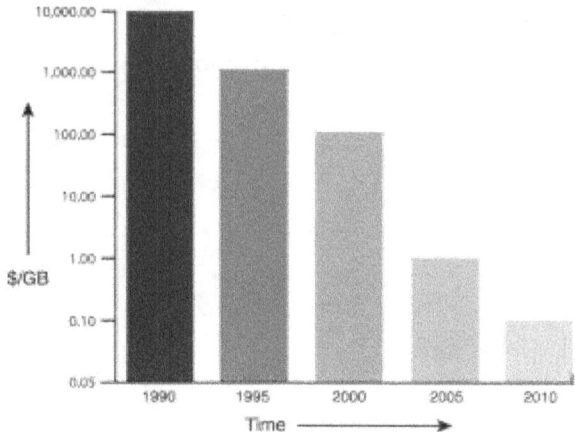

Figure 2.5 Data storage prices have dropped dramatically from more than $10,000 to less than $0.10 per GB over the decades.

Social Media

The emergence of social media has empowered customers to provide feedback in near-realtime via open and public mediums. This shift has forced businesses to consider customer feedback on their service and product offerings in their strategic planning. As a result, businesses are storing increasing amounts of data on customer interactions within their customer relationship management systems (CRM) and from harvesting customer reviews, complaints and praise from social media sites. This information feeds Big Data analysis algorithms that surface the voice of the customer in an attempt to provide better levels of service, increase sales, enable targeted marketing and even create new products and services. Businesses have realized that branding activity is no longer completely managed by internal marketing activities. Instead, product brands and corporate reputation are co-created by the company and its customers. For this reason, businesses are increasingly interested in incorporating publicly available datasets from social media and other external data sources.

Hyper-Connected Communities and Devices

The broadening coverage of the Internet and the proliferation of cellular and Wi-Fi networks has enabled more people and their devices to be continuously active in virtual communities. Coupled with the proliferation of Internet connected sensors, the underpinnings of the Internet of Things (IoT), a vast collection of smart Internet-connected devices, is being formed. As shown in Figure 2.6, this in turn has resulted in a massive increase in the number of available data streams. While some streams are public, other streams are channeled directly to corporations for analysis. As an example, the performance-based management contracts associated with heavy equipment used in the mining industry incentivize the optimal performance of preventive and predictive maintenance in an effort to reduce the need and avoid the downtime associated with unplanned corrective maintenance. This requires detailed analysis of sensor readings emitted by the equipment for the early detection of issues that can be resolved via the proactive scheduling of maintenance activities.

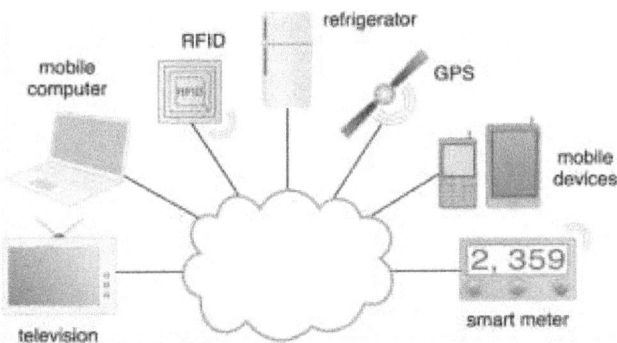

Figure 2.6 Hyper-connected communities and devices include television, mobile computing, RFIDs, refrigerators, GPS devices, mobile devices and smart meters.

Cloud Computing

Cloud computing advancements have led to the creation of environments that are capable of providing highly scalable, on-demand IT resources that can be leased via pay-as-you-go models. Businesses have the opportunity to leverage the infrastructure, storage and processing capabilities provided by these environments in order to build-out scalable Big Data solutions that can carry out large-scale processing tasks. Although traditionally thought of as off-premise environments typically depicted with a cloud symbol, businesses are also leveraging cloud management software to create on premise clouds to more effectively utilize their existing infrastructure via virtualization. In either case, the ability of a cloud to dynamically scale based upon load allows for the creation of resilient analytic environments that maximize efficient utilization of ICT resources.

Figure 2.7 displays an example of how a cloud environment can be leveraged for its scaling capabilities to perform Big Data processing tasks. The fact that off-premise cloud-based IT resources can be leased dramatically reduces the required up-front investment of Big Data projects.

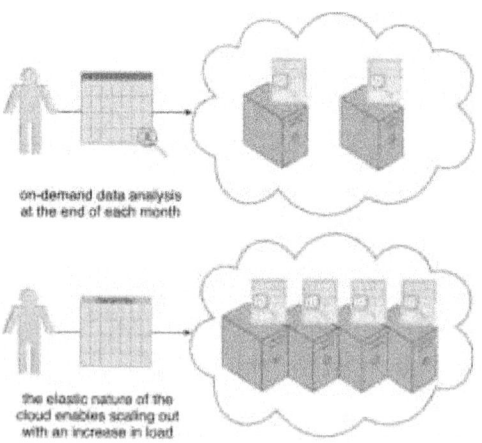

Figure 2.7 The cloud can be used to complete on-demand data analysis at the end of each month or enable the scaling out of systems with an increase in load.

It makes sense for enterprises already using cloud computing to reuse the cloud for their

Big Data initiatives because:

- Personnel already possesses the required cloud computing skills
- the input data already exists in the cloud

Migrating to the cloud is logical for enterprises planning to run analytics on datasets that are available via data markets, as many data markets make their datasets available in a cloud environment, such as Amazon S3.

In short, cloud computing can provide three essential ingredients required for a Big Data solution: external datasets, scalable processing capabilities and vast amounts of storage.

2.5 Internet of Everything (IoE)

The convergence of advancements in information and communications technology, marketplace dynamics, business architecture and business process management all contribute to the opportunity of what is now known as the Internet of Everything or IoE. The IoE combines the services provided by smart connected devices of the Internet of Things into meaningful business processes that possess the ability to provide unique and differentiating value propositions. It is a platform for innovation enabling the creation of new products and services and new sources of revenue for businesses. Big Data is the heart of the IoE. Hyper-connected communities and devices running on affordable technology and commodity hardware stream digitized data that is subject to analytic processes hosted in elastic cloud computing environments. The results of the analysis can provide insight as to how much value is generated by the current process and whether or not the process should proactively seek opportunities to further optimize itself.

IoE-specific companies can leverage Big Data to establish and optimize workflows and offer them to third parties as outsourced business processes. As established in the Business Process Manifesto edited by Roger Burlton (2011), an organization's business processes are the source for generating outcomes of value for customers and other stakeholders. In combination with the analysis of streaming data and customer context, being able to adapt the execution of these processes to align with the customer's goals will be a key corporate differentiator in the future.

One example of an area that has benefited from the IoE is precision agriculture, with traditional farming equipment manufacturers leading the way. When joined together as a system of systems, GPS-controlled tractors, in-field moisture and fertilization sensors, on-demand watering, fertilization, pesticide application systems and variable rate seeding equipment can maximize field productivity while minimizing cost. Precision agriculture enables alternative farming approaches that challenge industrial monoculture farms. With the aid of the IoE, smaller farms are able to compete by leveraging crop diversity and environmentally sensitive practices. Besides having smart connected farming equipment, the Big Data analysis of equipment and in-field sensor data can drive a decision support system that can guide farmers and their machines to optimum yields.

Chapter III

Big Data Adoption and Planning Considerations

Big Data initiatives are strategic in nature and should be business-driven. The adoption of Big Data can be transformative but is more often innovative. Transformation activities are typically low-risk endeavors designed to deliver increased efficiency and effectiveness.

Innovation requires a shift in mindset because it will fundamentally alter the structure of a business either in its products, services or organization. This is the power of Big Data adoption; it can enable this sort of change. Innovation management requires care—too many controlling forces can stifle the initiative and dampen the results, and too little oversight can turn a best intentioned project into a science experiment that never delivers promised results. It is against this backdrop that Chapter 3 addresses Big Data adoption and planning considerations.

Given the nature of Big Data and its analytic power, there are many issues that need to be considered and planned for in the beginning. For example, with the adoption of any new technology, the means to secure it in a way that conforms to existing corporate standards needs to be addressed. Issues related to tracking the provenance of a dataset from its procurement to its utilization is often a new requirement for organizations. Managing the privacy of constituents whose data is being handled or whose identity is revealed by analytic processes must be planned for. Big Data even opens up additional opportunities to consider moving beyond on-premise environments and into remotely-provisioned, scalable environments that are hosted in a cloud. In fact, all of the above considerations require an organization to recognize and establish a set of distinct governance processes and decision frameworks to ensure that responsible parties understand Big Data's nature, implications and management requirements.

Organizationally, the adoption of Big Data changes the approach to performing business analytics. For this reason, a Big Data analytics lifecycle is introduced in this chapter. The lifecycle begins with the establishment of a business case for the Big Data project and ends with ensuring that the analytic results are deployed to the organization to generate maximal value. There are a number of stages in between that organize the steps of identifying, procuring, filtering, extracting, cleansing and aggregating of data. This is all required before the analysis even occurs. The execution of this lifecycle requires new competencies to be developed or hired into the organization.

As demonstrated, there are many things to consider and account for when adopting Big Data. This chapter explains the primary potential issues and considerations.

3.1 Organization Prerequisites

Big Data frameworks are not turn-key solutions. In order for data analysis and analytics to offer value, enterprises need to have data management and Big Data governance frameworks. Sound processes and sufficient skillsets for those who will be responsible for implementing, customizing, populating and using Big Data solutions are also necessary. Additionally, the quality of the data targeted for processing by Big Data solutions needs to be assessed.

Outdated, invalid, or poorly identified data will result in low-quality input which, regardless of how good the Big Data solution is, will continue to produce low-quality results. The longevity of the Big Data environment also needs to be planned for. A roadmap needs to be defined to ensure that any necessary expansion or augmentation of the environment is planned out to stay in sync with the requirements of the enterprise.

3.2 Data Procurement

The acquisition of Big Data solutions themselves can be economical, due to the availability of open-source platforms and tools and opportunities to leverage commodity hardware. However, a substantial budget may still be required to obtain external data. The nature of the business may make external data very valuable. The greater the volume and variety of data that can be supplied, the higher the chances are of finding hidden insights from patterns.

External data sources include government data sources and commercial data markets. Government-provided data, such as geo-spatial data, may be free. However, most commercially relevant data will need to be purchased and may involve the continuation of subscription costs to ensure the delivery of updates to procured datasets.

3.3 Privacy

Performing analytics on datasets can reveal confidential information about organizations or individuals. Even analyzing separate datasets that contain seemingly benign data can reveal private information when the datasets are analyzed jointly. This can lead to intentional or inadvertent breaches of privacy.

Addressing these privacy concerns requires an understanding of the nature of data being accumulated and relevant data privacy regulations, as well as special techniques for data tagging and anonymization. For example, telemetry data, such as a car's GPS log or smart meter data readings, collected over an extended period of time can reveal an individual's location and behavior, as shown in Figure 3.1.

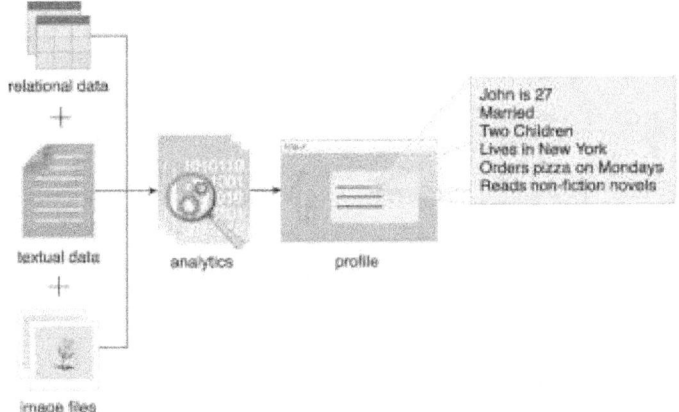

Figure 3.1 Information gathered from running analytics on image files, relational data and textual data is used to create John's profile.

3.4 Security

Some of the components of Big Data solutions lack the robustness of traditional enterprise solution environments when it comes to access control and data security. Securing Big Data involves ensuring that the data networks and repositories are sufficiently secured via authentication and authorization mechanisms.

Big Data security further involves establishing data access levels for different categories of users. For example, unlike traditional relational database management systems, NoSQL databases generally do not provide robust built-in security mechanisms. They instead rely on simple HTTP-based APIs where data is exchanged in plaintext, making the data prone to network-based attacks, as shown in Figure 3.2.

Figure 3.2 NoSQL databases can be susceptible to network-based attacks.

3.5 Provenance

Provenance refers to information about the source of the data and how it has been processed. Provenance information helps determine the authenticity and quality of data, and it can be used for auditing purposes. Maintaining provenance as large volumes of data are acquired, combined and put through multiple processing stages can be a complex task. At different stages in the analytics lifecycle, data will be in different states due to the fact it may be being transmitted, processed or in storage. These states correspond to the notion of data-in-motion, data-in-use and data-at-rest. Importantly, whenever Big Data changes state, it should trigger the capture of provenance information that is recorded as metadata.

As data enters the analytic environment, its provenance record can be initialized with the recording of information that captures the pedigree of the data. Ultimately, the goal of capturing provenance is to be able to reason over the generated analytic results with the knowledge of the origin of the data and what steps or algorithms were used to process the data that led to the result. Provenance information is essential to being able to realize the value of the analytic result. Much like scientific research, if results cannot be justified and repeated, they lack credibility. When provenance information is captured on the way to generating analytic results as in Figure 3.3, the results can be more easily trusted and thereby used with confidence.

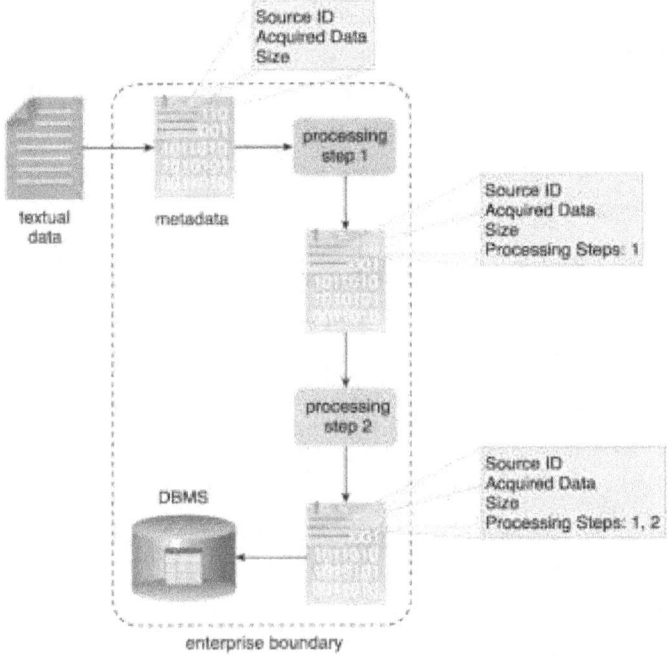

Figure 3.3 Data may also need to be annotated with source dataset attributes and processing step details as it passes through the data transformation steps.

3.6 Limited Realtime Support

Dashboards and other applications that require streaming data and alerts often demand realtime or near-realtime data transmissions. Many open source Big Data solutions and tools are batch-oriented; however, there is a new generation of realtime capable open source tools that have support for streaming data analysis. Many of the realtime data analysis solutions that do exist are proprietary. Approaches that achieve near-realtime results often process transactional data as it arrives and combine it with previously summarized batch-processed data.

3.7 Distinct Performance Challenges

Due to the volumes of data that some Big Data solutions are required to process, performance is often a concern. For example, large datasets coupled with complex search algorithms can lead to long query times. Another performance challenge is related to network bandwidth. With increasing data volumes, the time to transfer a unit of data can exceed its actual data processing time, as shown in Figure 3.4.

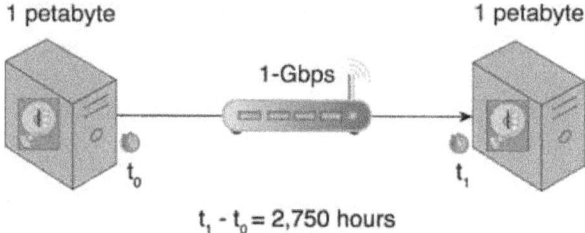

$t_1 - t_0 = 2{,}750$ hours

Figure 3.4 Transferring 1 PB of data via a 1-Gigabit LAN connection at 80% throughput will take approximately 2,750 hours.

3.8 Distinct Governance Requirements

Big Data solutions access data and generate data, all of which become assets of the business. A governance framework is required to ensure that the data and the solution environment itself are regulated, standardized and evolved in a controlled manner.

Examples of what a Big Data governance framework can encompass include:

- Standardization of how data is tagged and the metadata used for tagging
- Policies that regulate the kind of external data that may be acquired
- Policies regarding the management of data privacy and data anonymization

- Policies for the archiving of data sources and analysis results
- Policies that establish guidelines for data cleansing and filtering

3.9 Distinct Methodology

A methodology will be required to control how data flows into and out of Big Data solutions. It will need to consider how feedback loops can be established to enable the processed data to undergo repeated refinement, as shown in Figure 3.5. For example, an iterative approach may be used to enable business personnel to provide IT personnel with feedback on a periodic basis. Each feedback cycle provides opportunities for system refinement by modifying data preparation or data analysis steps.

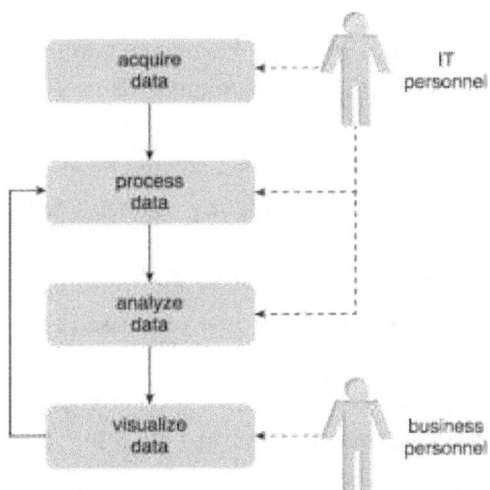

Figure 3.5 Each repetition can help fine-tune processing steps, algorithms and data models to improve the accuracy of results and deliver greater value to the business.

3.10 Clouds

As mentioned in Chapter 2, clouds provide remote environments that can host IT infrastructure for large-scale storage and processing, among other things. Regardless of whether an organization is already cloud-enabled, the adoption of a Big Data environment may necessitate that some or all of that environment be hosted within a cloud. For example, an enterprise that runs its CRM system in a cloud decides to add a Big Data solution in the same cloud environment in order to run analytics on its CRM data. This data can then be shared with its primary Big Data environment that resides within the enterprise boundaries.

Common justifications for incorporating a cloud environment in support of a Big Data solution include:

- Inadequate in-house hardware resources
- Upfront capital investment for system procurement is not available
- The project is to be isolated from the rest of the business so that existing business processes are not impacted
- The big data initiative is a proof of concept
- Datasets that need to be processed are already cloud resident
- The limits of available computing and storage resources used by an in-house big data solution are being reached

3.11 Big Data Analytics Lifecycle

Big Data analysis differs from traditional data analysis primarily due to the volume, velocity and variety characteristics of the data being processes. To address the distinct requirements for performing analysis on Big Data, a step-by-step methodology is needed to organize the activities and tasks involved with acquiring, processing, analyzing and repurposing data. The upcoming sections explore a specific data analytics lifecycle that organizes and manages the tasks and activities associated with the analysis of Big Data. From a Big Data adoption and planning perspective, it is important that in addition to the lifecycle, consideration be made for issues of training, education, tooling and staffing of a data analytics team.

The Big Data analytics lifecycle can be divided into the following nine stages, as shown in

Figure 3.6:

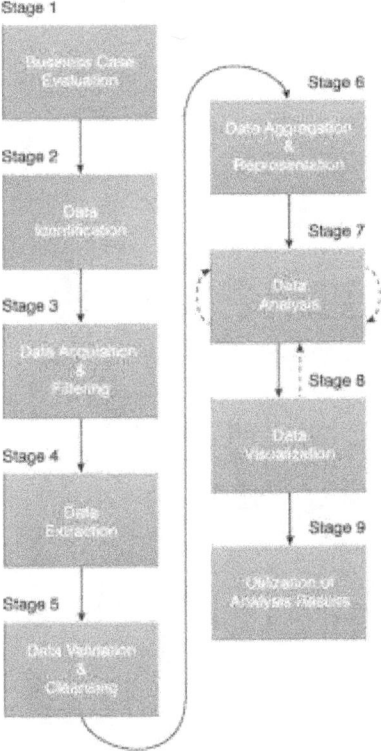

1. Business Case Evaluation
2. Data Identification
3. Data Acquisition & Filtering

4. Data Extraction
5. Data Validation & Cleansing
6. Data Aggregation & Representation
7. Data Analysis
8. Data Visualization
9. Utilization of Analysis Results

Business Case Evaluation

Each Big Data analytics lifecycle must begin with a well-defined business case that presents a clear understanding of the justification, motivation and goals of carrying out the analysis. The Business Case Evaluation stage shown in Figure 3.7 requires that a business case be created, assessed and approved prior to proceeding with the actual hands-on analysis tasks.

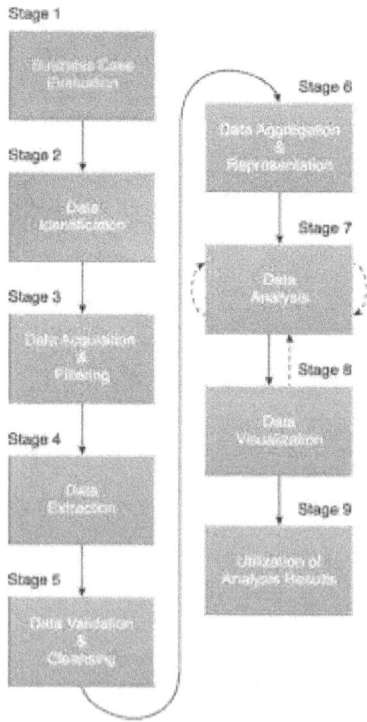

Figure 3.7 Stage 1 of the Big Data analytics lifecycle.

An evaluation of a Big Data analytics business case helps decision-makers understand the business resources that will need to be utilized and which business challenges the analysis will tackle. The further identification of KPIs during this stage can help determine assessment criteria and guidance for the evaluation of the analytic results. If KPIs are not readily available, efforts should be made to make the goals of the analysis project SMART, which stands for specific, measurable, attainable, relevant and timely.

Based on business requirements that are documented in the business case, it can be determined whether the business problems being addressed are really Big Data problems. In order to qualify as a Big Data problem, a business problem needs to be directly related to one or more of the Big Data characteristics of volume, velocity, or variety.

Note also that another outcome of this stage is the determination of the underlying budget required to carry out the analysis project. Any required purchase, such as tools, hardware and training, must be understood in advance so that the anticipated investment can be weighed against the expected benefits of achieving the goals. Initial iterations of the Big Data analytics lifecycle will require more up-front investment of Big Data technologies, products and training compared to later iterations where these earlier investments can be repeatedly leveraged.

Data Identification

The Data Identification stage shown in Figure 3.8 is dedicated to identifying the datasets required for the analysis project and their sources.

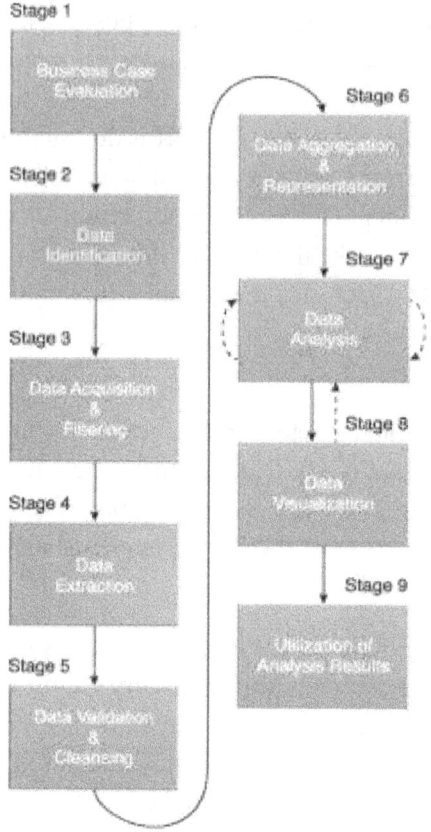

Figure 3.8 Data Identification is stage 2 of the Big Data analytics lifecycle.

Identifying a wider variety of data sources may increase the probability of finding hidden patterns and correlations. For example, to provide insight, it can be beneficial to identify as many types of related data sources as possible, especially when it is unclear exactly what to look for.

Depending on the business scope of the analysis project and nature of the business problems being addressed, the required datasets and their sources can be internal and/or external to the enterprise.

In the case of internal datasets, a list of available datasets from internal sources, such as data marts and operational systems, are typically compiled and matched against a pre-defined dataset specification.

In the case of external datasets, a list of possible third-party data providers, such as data markets and publicly available datasets, are compiled. Some forms of external data may be embedded within blogs or other types of content-based web sites, in which case they may need to be harvested via automated tools.

Data Acquisition and Filtering

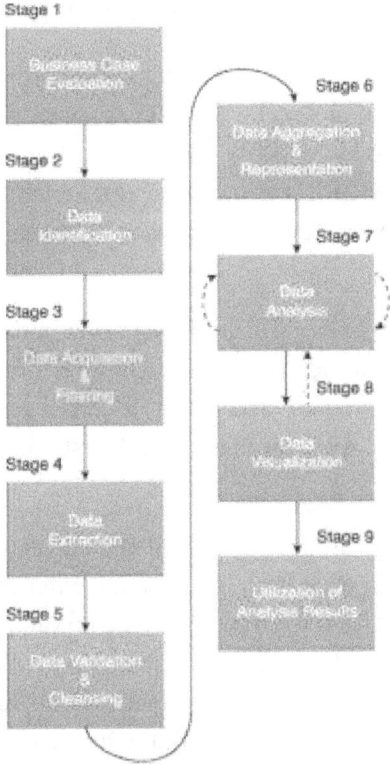

Figure 3.9 Stage 3 of the Big Data analytics lifecycle.

During the Data Acquisition and Filtering stage, shown in Figure 3.9, the data is gathered from all of the data sources that were identified during the previous stage. The acquired data is then subjected to automated filtering for the removal of corrupt data or data that has been deemed to have no value to the analysis objectives.

Depending on the type of data source, data may come as a collection of files, such as data purchased from a third-party data provider, or may require API integration, such as with Twitter. In many cases, especially where external, unstructured data is concerned, some or most of the acquired data may be irrelevant (noise) and can be discarded as part of the filtering process.

Data classified as "corrupt" can include records with missing or nonsensical values or invalid data types. Data that is filtered out for one analysis may possibly be valuable for a different type of analysis. Therefore, it is advisable to store a verbatim copy of the original dataset before proceeding with the filtering. To minimize the required storage space, the verbatim copy can be compressed.

Both internal and external data needs to be persisted once it gets generated or enters the enterprise boundary. For batch analytics, this data is persisted to disk prior to analysis. In the case of realtime analytics, the data is analyzed first and then persisted to disk.

As evidenced in Figure 3.10, metadata can be added via automation to data from both internal and external data sources to improve the classification and querying. Examples of appended metadata include dataset size and structure, source information, date and time of creation or collection and language-specific information. It is vital that metadata be machine-readable and passed forward along subsequent analysis stages. This helps maintain data provenance throughout the Big Data analytics lifecycle, which helps to establish and preserve data accuracy and quality.

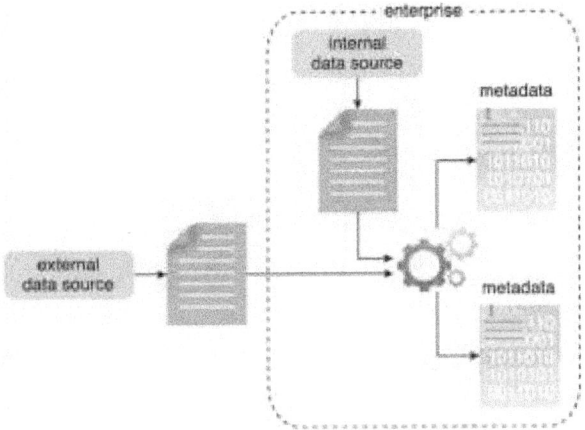

Figure 3.10 Metadata is added to data from internal and external sources.

Data Extraction

Some of the data identified as input for the analysis may arrive in a format incompatible with the Big Data solution. The need to address disparate types of data is more likely with data from external sources. The Data Extraction lifecycle stage, shown in Figure 3.11, is dedicated to extracting disparate data and transforming it into a format that the underlying Big Data solution can use for the purpose of the data analysis.

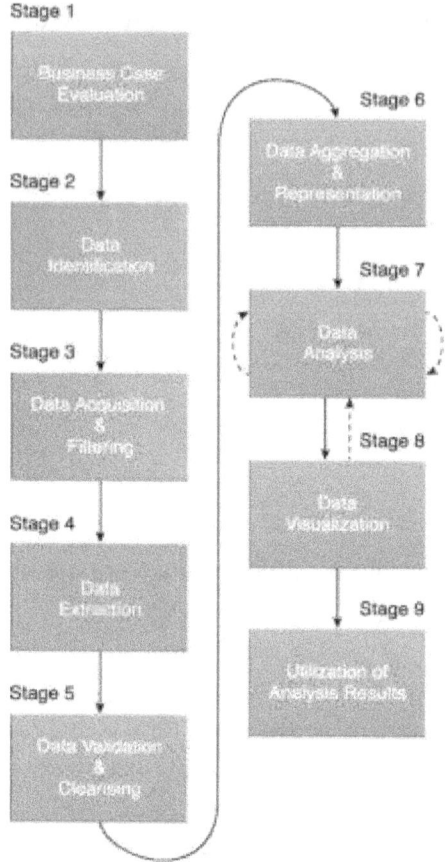

Figure 3.11 Stage 4 of the Big Data analytics lifecycle.

The extent of extraction and transformation required depends on the types of analytics and capabilities of the Big Data solution. For example, extracting the required fields from delimited textual data, such as with webserver log files, may not be necessary if the underlying Big Data solution can already directly process those files.

Similarly, extracting text for text analytics, which requires scans of whole documents, is simplified if the underlying Big Data solution can directly read the document in its native format.

Figure 3.12 illustrates the extraction of comments and a user ID embedded within an XML document without the need for further transformation.

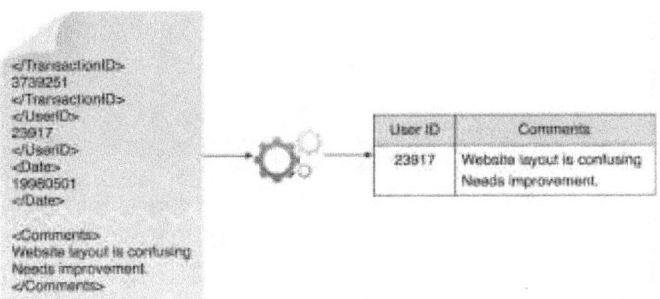

Figure 3.12 Comments and user IDs are extracted from an XML document.

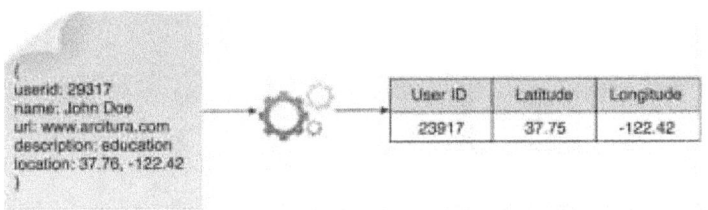

Figure 3.13 demonstrates the extraction of the latitude and longitude coordinates of a user from a single JSON field.

Figure 3.13 The user ID and coordinates of a user are extracted from a single JSON field.

Further transformation is needed in order to separate the data into two separate fields as required by the Big Data solution.

Data Validation and Cleansing

Invalid data can skew and falsify analysis results. Unlike traditional enterprise data, where the data structure is pre-defined and data is pre-validated, data input into Big Data analyses can be unstructured without any indication of validity. Its complexity can further make it difficult to arrive at a set of suitable validation constraints.

The Data Validation and Cleansing stage shown in Figure 3.14 is dedicated to establishing often complex validation rules and removing any known invalid data.

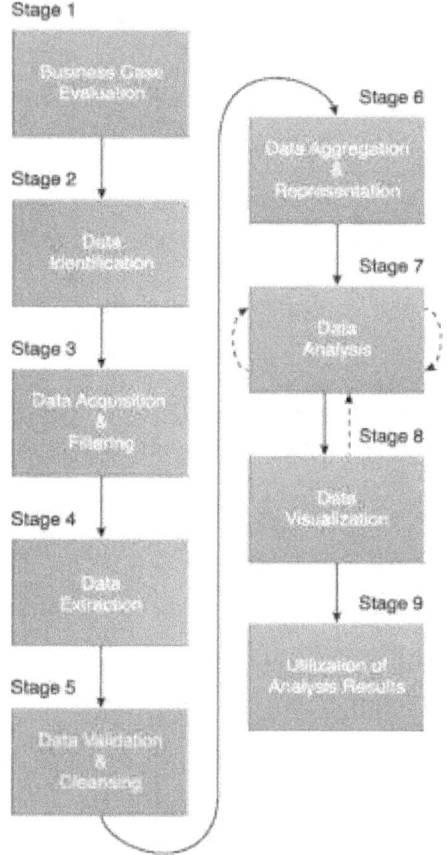

Figure 3.14 Stage 5 of the Big Data analytics lifecycle.

Big Data solutions often receive redundant data across different datasets. This redundancy can be exploited to explore interconnected datasets in order to assemble validation parameters and fill in missing valid data.

For example, as illustrated in Figure 3.15:

- The first value in Dataset B is validated against its corresponding value in Dataset A.
- The second value in Dataset B is not validated against its corresponding value in Dataset A.
- If a value is missing, it is inserted from Dataset A.

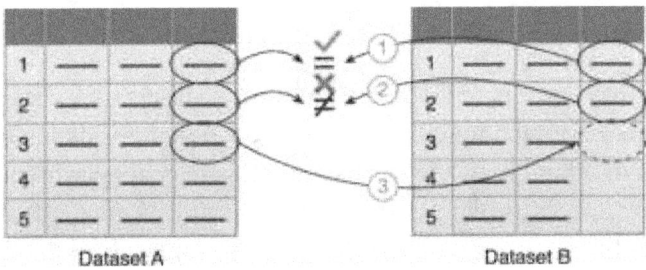

Figure 3.15 Data validation can be used to examine interconnected datasets in order to fill in missing valid data.

For batch analytics, data validation and cleansing can be achieved via an offline ETL operation. For realtime analytics, a more complex in-memory system is required to validate and cleanse the data as it arrives from the source. Provenance can play an important role in determining the accuracy and quality of questionable data. Data that appears to be invalid may still be valuable in that it may possess hidden patterns and trends, as shown in Figure 3.16.

Figure 3.16 The presence of invalid data is resulting in spikes. Although the data appears abnormal, it may be indicative of a new pattern.

Data Aggregation and Representation

Data may be spread across multiple datasets, requiring that datasets be joined together via common fields, for example date or ID. In other cases, the same data fields may appear in multiple datasets, such as date of birth. Either way, a method of data reconciliation is required or the dataset representing the correct value needs to be determined.

The Data Aggregation and Representation stage, shown in Figure 3.17, is dedicated to integrating multiple datasets together to arrive at a unified view.

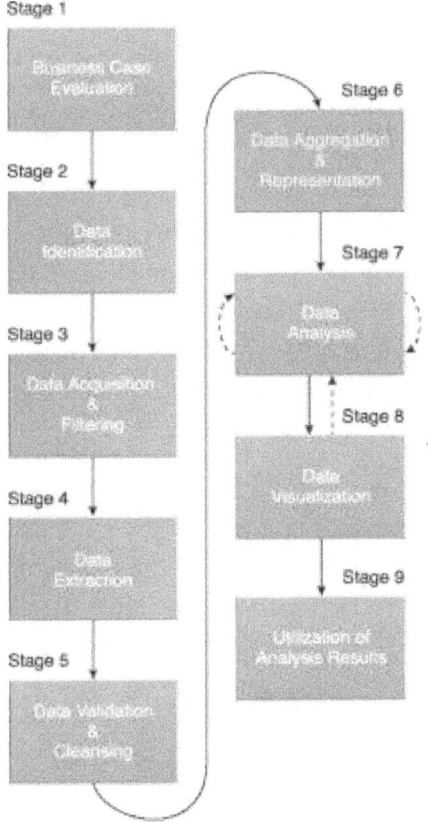

Figure 3.17 Stage 6 of the Big Data analytics lifecycle.

Performing this stage can become complicated because of differences in:

- Data Structure – Although the data format may be the same, the data model may be different.
- Semantics – A value that is labeled differently in two different datasets may mean the same thing, for example "surname" and "last name."

The large volumes processed by Big Data solutions can make data aggregation a time and effort-intensive operation. Reconciling these differences can require complex logic that is executed automatically without the need for human intervention.

Future data analysis requirements need to be considered during this stage to help foster data reusability. Whether data aggregation is required or not, it is important to understand that the same data can be stored in many different forms. One form may be better suited for a particular type of analysis than another. For example, data stored as a BLOB would be of little use if the analysis requires access to individual data fields.

A data structure standardized by the Big Data solution can act as a common denominator that can be used for a range of analysis techniques and projects. This can require establishing a central, standard analysis repository, such as a NoSQL database, as shown in Figure 3.18.

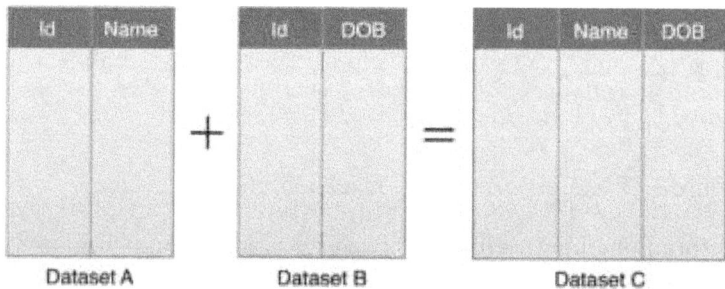

Figure 3.18 A simple example of data aggregation where two datasets are aggregated together using the Id field.

Figure 3.19 shows the same piece of data stored in two different formats. Dataset A contains the desired piece of data, but it is part of a BLOB that is not readily accessible for querying. Dataset B contains the same piece of data organized in column-based storage, enabling each field to be queried individually.

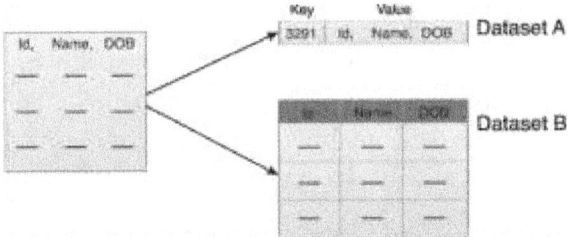

Figure 3.19 Dataset A and B can be combined to create a standardized data structure with a Big Data solution.

Data Analysis

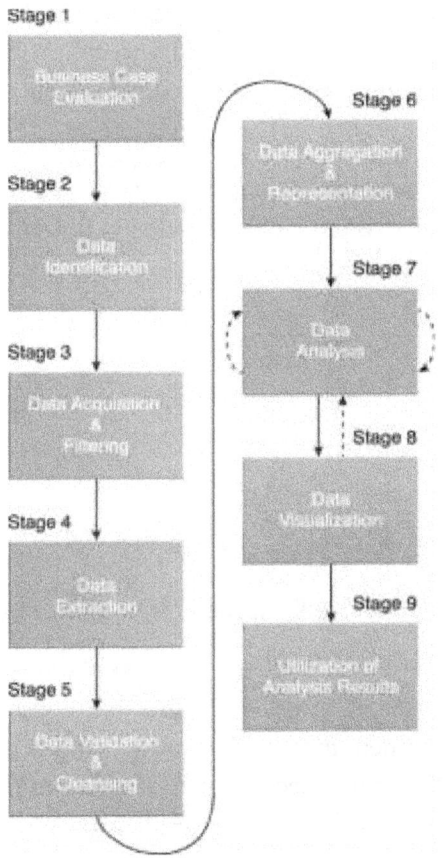

Figure 3.20 Stage 7 of the Big Data analytics lifecycle.

The Data Analysis stage shown in Figure 3.20 is dedicated to carrying out the actual analysis task, which typically involves one or more types of analytics. This stage can be iterative in nature, especially if the data analysis is exploratory, in which case analysis is repeated until the appropriate pattern or correlation is uncovered. The exploratory analysis approach will be explained shortly, along with confirmatory analysis.

Depending on the type of analytic result required, this stage can be as simple as querying a dataset to compute an aggregation for comparison. On the other hand, it can be as challenging as combining data mining and complex statistical analysis techniques to discover patterns and anomalies or to generate a statistical or mathematical model to depict relationships between variables.

Data analysis can be classified as confirmatory analysis or exploratory analysis, the latter of which is linked to data mining, as shown in Figure 3.21.

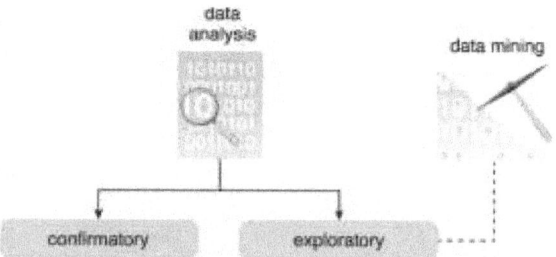

Figure 3.21 Data analysis can be carried out as confirmatory or exploratory analysis.

Confirmatory data analysis is a deductive approach where the cause of the phenomenon being investigated is proposed beforehand. The proposed cause or assumption is called a hypothesis. The data is then analyzed to prove or disprove the hypothesis and provide definitive answers to specific questions. Data sampling techiniques are typically used. Unexpected findings or anomalies are usually ignored since a predetermined cause was assumed.

Exploratory data analysis is an inductive approach that is closely associated with data mining. No hypothesis or predetermined assumptions are generated. Instead, the data is explored through analysis to develop an understanding of the cause of the phenomenon. Although it may not provide definitive answers, this method provides a general direction that can facilitate the discovery of patterns or anomalies.

Data Visualization

The ability to analyze massive amounts of data and find useful insights carries little value if the only ones that can interpret the results are the analysts.

The Data Visualization stage, shown in Figure 3.22, is dedicated to using data visualization techniques and tools to graphically communicate the analysis results for effective interpretation by business users.

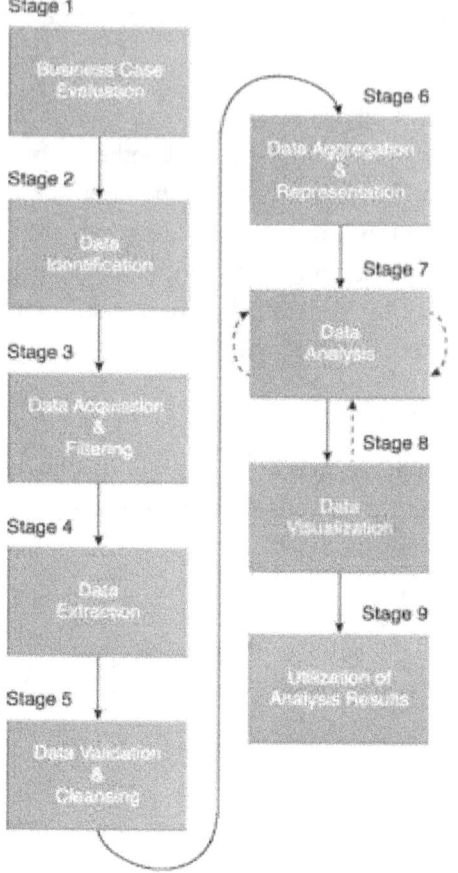

Figure 3.22 Stage 8 of the Big Data analytics lifecycle.

Business users need to be able to understand the results in order to obtain value from the analysis and subsequently have the ability to provide feedback, as indicated by the dashed line leading from stage 8 back to stage 7.

The results of completing the Data Visualization stage provide users with the ability to perform visual analysis, allowing for the discovery of answers to questions that users have not yet even formulated. Visual analysis techniques are covered later in this book.

The same results may be presented in a number of different ways, which can influence the interpretation of the results. Consequently, it is important to use the most suitable visualization technique by keeping the business domain in context.

Another aspect to keep in mind is that providing a method of drilling down to comparatively simple statistics is crucial, in order for users to understand how the rolled up or aggregated results were generated.

Utilization of Analysis Results

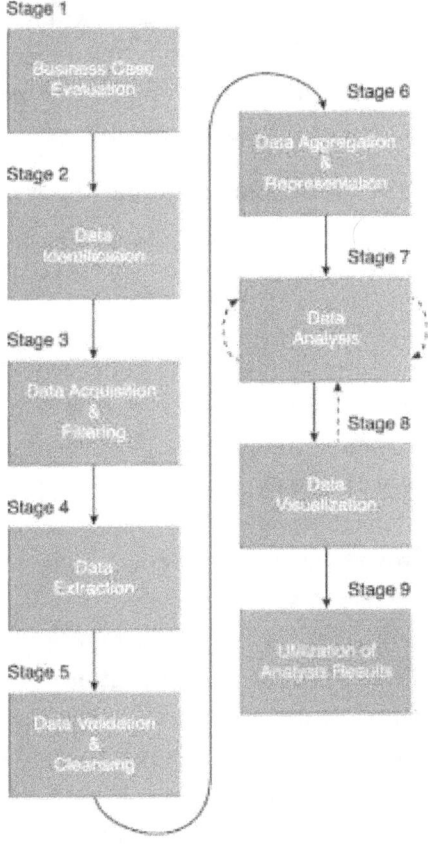

Figure 3.23 Stage 9 of the Big Data analytics lifecycle.

Subsequent to analysis results being made available to business users to support business decision-making, such as via dashboards, there may be further opportunities to utilize the analysis results. The Utilization of Analysis Results stage, shown in Figure 3.23, is dedicated to determining how and where processed analysis data can be further leveraged.

Depending on the nature of the analysis problems being addressed, it is possible for the analysis results to produce "models" that encapsulate new insights and understandings about the nature of the patterns and relationships that exist within the data that was analyzed. A model may look like a mathematical equation or a set of rules. Models can be used to improve business process logic and application system logic, and they can form the basis of a new system or software program.

Common areas that are explored during this stage include the following:

- Input for Enterprise Systems – The data analysis results may be automatically or manually fed directly into enterprise systems to enhance and optimize their behaviors and performance. For example, an online store can be fed processed customer-related analysis results that may impact how it generates product recommendations. New models may be used to improve the programming logic within existing enterprise systems or may form the basis of new systems.
- Business Process Optimization – The identified patterns, correlations and anomalies discovered during the data analysis are used to refine business processes. An example is consolidating transportation routes as part of a supply chain process. Models may also lead to opportunities to improve business process logic.

- Alerts – Data analysis results can be used as input for existing alerts or may form the basis of new alerts. For example, alerts may be created to inform users via email or SMS text about an event that requires them to take corrective action.

Chapter IV

Enterprise Technologies and Big Data Business Intelligence Clusters

As described in Chapter 2, in an enterprise executed as a layered system, the strategic layer constrains the tactical layer, which directs the operational layer. The alignment of layers is captured through metrics and performance indicators, which provide the operational layer with insight into how its processes are executing. These measurements are aggregated and enhanced with additional meaning to become KPIs, through which managers of the tactical layer can assess corporate performance, or business execution. The KPIs are related with other measurements and understandings that are used to assess critical success factors. Ultimately, this series of enrichment corresponds with the transformation of data into information, information into knowledge and knowledge into wisdom.

This chapter discusses the enterprise technologies that support this transformation. Data is held within the operational-level information systems of an organization. Moreover, database structure is leveraged with queries to generate information. Higher up the analytic food chain are analytical processing systems. These systems leverage multi-dimensional structures to answer more complex queries and provide deeper insight into business operations. On a larger scale, data is collected from throughout the enterprise and warehoused in a data warehouse. It is from these data stores that management gains insight into broader corporate performance and KPIs.

4.1 Online Transaction Processing (OLTP)

OLTP is a software system that processes transaction-oriented data. The term "online transaction" refers to the completion of an activity in realtime and is not batch-processed. OLTP systems store operational data that is normalized. This data is a common source of structured data and serves as input to many analytic processes. Big Data analysis results can be used to augment OLTP data stored in the underlying relational databases. OLTP systems, for example a point of sale system, execute business processes in support of corporate operations. As shown in Figure 4.1, they perform transactions against a relational database.

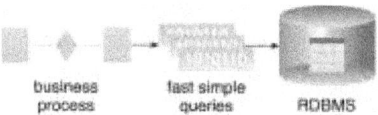

Figure 4.1 OLTP systems perform simple database operations to provide sub-second response times.

The queries supported by OLTP systems are comprised of simple insert, delete and update operations with sub-second response times. Examples include ticket reservation systems, banking and point of sale systems.

4.2 Online Analytical Processing (OLAP)

Online analytical processing (OLAP) systems are used for processing data analysis queries. OLAPs form an integral part of business intelligence, data mining and machine learning processes. They are relevant to Big Data in that they can serve as both a data source as well as a data sink that is capable of receiving data. They are used in diagnostic, predictive and prescriptive analytics. As shown in Figure 4.2, OLAP systems perform long-running, complex queries against a multidimensional database whose structure is optimized for performing advanced analytics.

Figure 4.2 OLAP systems use multidimensional databases.

OLAP systems store historical data that is aggregated and denormalized to support fast reporting capability. They further use databases that store historical data in multidimensional structures and can answer complex queries based on the relationships between multiple aspects of the data.

4.3 Extract Transform Load (ETL)

Extract Transform Load (ETL) is a process of loading data from a source system into a target system. The source system can be a database, a flat file, or an application. Similarly, the target system can be a database or some other storage system.

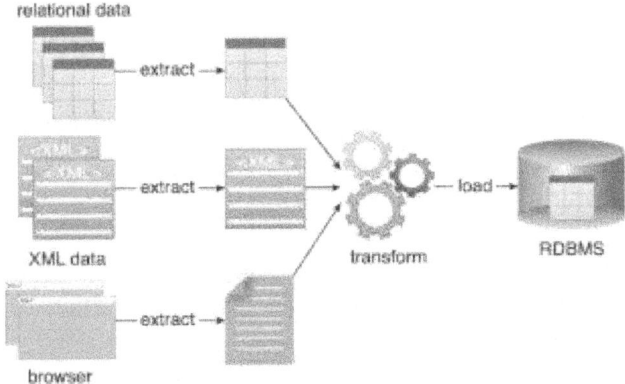

Figure 4.3 An ETL process can extract data from multiple sources and transform it for loading into a single target system.

ETL represents the main operation through which data warehouses are fed data. A Big Data solution encompasses the ETL feature-set for converting data of different types. Figure 4.3

shows that the required data is first obtained or extracted from the sources, after which the extracts are modified or transformed by the application of rules. Finally, the data is inserted or loaded into the target system.

4.4 Data Warehouses

A data warehouse is a central, enterprise-wide repository consisting of historical and current data. Data warehouses are heavily used by BI to run various analytical queries, and they usually interface with an OLAP system to support multi-dimensional analytical queries, as shown in Figure 4.4.

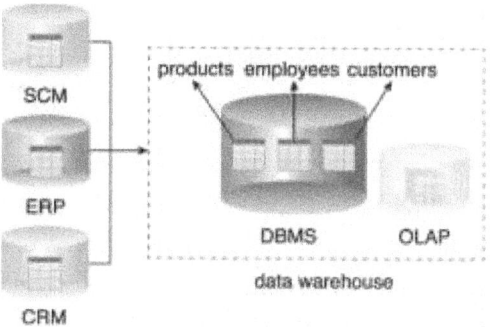

Figure 4.4 Batch jobs periodically load data into a data warehouse from operational systems like ERP, CRM and SCM.

Data pertaining to multiple business entities from different operational systems is periodically extracted, validated, transformed and consolidated into a single deformalized database. With periodic data imports from across the enterprise, the amount of data contained in a given data warehouse will continue to increase. Over time this leads to slower query response times for data analysis tasks. To resolve this shortcoming, data warehouses usually contain optimized databases, called analytical databases, to handle reporting and data analysis tasks. An analytical database can exist as a separate DBMS, as in the case of an OLAP database.

4.5 Data Marts

A data mart is a subset of the data stored in a data warehouse that typically belongs to a department, division, or specific line of business. Data warehouses can have multiple data marts. As shown in Figure 4.5, enterprise-wide data is collected and business entities are then extracted. Domain-specific entities are persisted into the data warehouse via an ETL process.

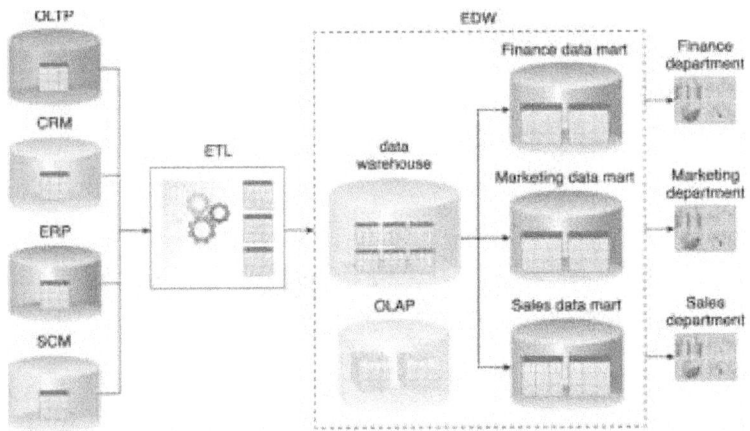

Figure 4.5 A data warehouse's single version of "truth" is based on cleansed data, which is a prerequisite for accurate and error-free reports, as per the output shown on the right.

4.6 Traditional BI

Traditional BI primarily utilizes descriptive and diagnostic analytics to provide information on historical and current events. It is not "intelligent" because it only provides answers to correctly formulated questions. Correctly formulating questions requires an understanding of business problems and issues and of the data itself. BI reports on different KPIs through:

- ad-hoc reports
- dashboards

Ad-hoc Reports

Ad-hoc reporting is a process that involves manually processing data to produce custom-made reports, as shown in Figure 4.6. The focus of an ad-hoc report is usually on a specific area of the business, such as its marketing or supply chain management. The generated custom reports are detailed and often tabular in nature.

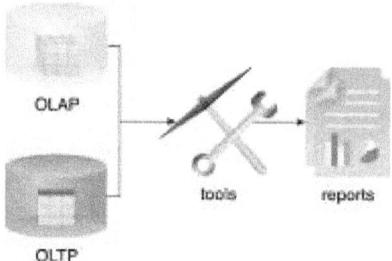

Figure 4.6 OLAP and OLTP data sources can be used by BI tools for both ad-hoc reporting and dashboards.

Dashboards

Dashboards provide a holistic view of key business areas. The information displayed on dashboards is generated at periodic intervals in realtime or near-realtime. The presentation of data on dashboards is graphical in nature, using bar charts, pie charts and gauges, as shown in Figure 4.7.

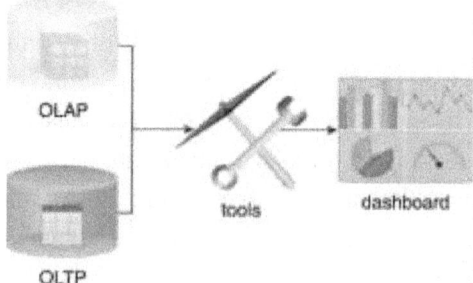

Figure 4.7 BI tools use both OLAP and OLTP to display the information on dashboards.

As previously explained, data warehouses and data marts contain consolidated and validated information about enterprise-wide business entities. Traditional BI cannot function effectively without data marts because they contain the optimized and segregated data that BI requires for reporting purposes. Without data marts, data needs to be extracted from the data warehouse via an ETL process on an ad-hoc basis whenever a query needs to be run. This increases the time and effort to execute queries and generate reports.

Traditional BI uses data warehouses and data marts for reporting and data analysis because they allow complex data analysis queries with multiple joins and aggregations to be issued, as shown in Figure 4.8.

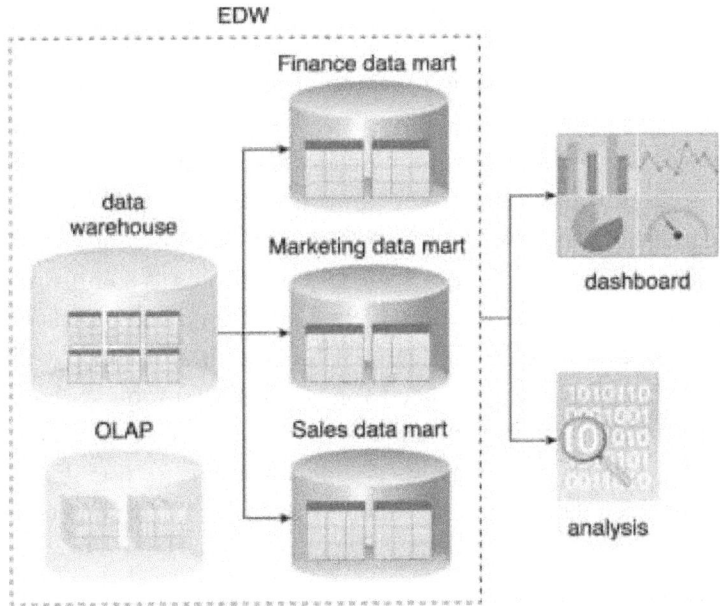

Figure 4.8 An example of traditional BI.

4.7 Big Data BIE

Big Data BI builds upon traditional BI by acting on the cleansed, consolidated enterprise-wide data in the data warehouse and combining it with semi-structured and unstructured data sources. It comprises both predictive and prescriptive analytics to facilitate the development of an enterprise-wide understanding of business performance.

While traditional BI analyses generally focus on individual business processes, Big Data BI analyses focus on multiple business processes simultaneously. This helps reveal patterns and anomalies across a broader scope within the enterprise. It also leads to data discovery by identifying insights and information that may have been previously absent or unknown.

Big Data BI requires the analysis of unstructured, semi-structured and structured data residing in the enterprise data warehouse. This requires a "next-generation" data warehouse that uses new features and technologies to store cleansed data originating from a variety of sources in a single uniform data format. The coupling of a traditional data warehouse with these new technologies results in a hybrid data warehouse. This warehouse acts as a uniform and central repository of structured, semi-structured and unstructured data that can provide Big Data BI tools with all of the required data. This eliminates the need for Big Data BI tools to have to connect to multiple data sources to retrieve or access data. In Figure 4.9, a next-generation data warehouse establishes a standardized data access layer across a range of data sources.

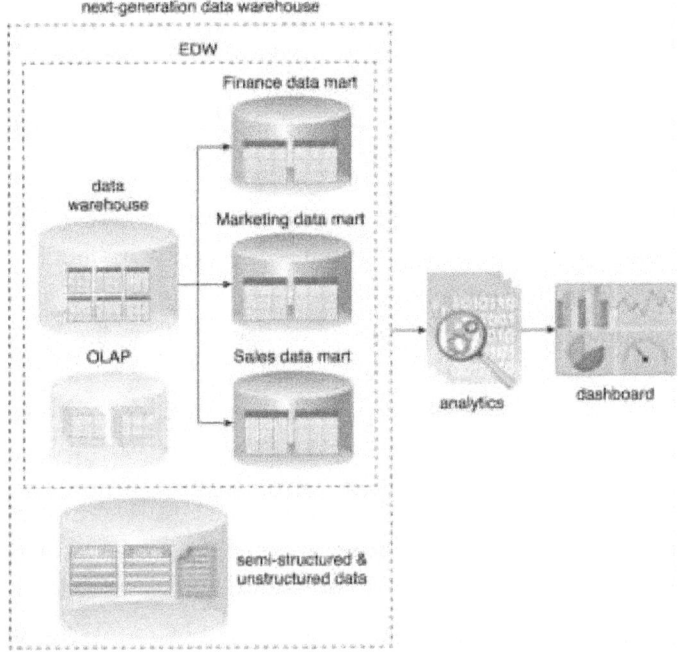

Figure 4.9 A next-generation data warehouse.

Traditional Data Visualization

Data visualization is a technique whereby analytical results are graphically communicated using elements like charts, maps, data grids, infographics and alerts. Graphically representing data can make it easier to understand reports, view trends and identify patterns.

Traditional data visualization provides mostly static charts and graphs in reports and dashboards, whereas contemporary data visualization tools are interactive and can provide both summarized and detailed views of data. They are designed to help people who lack statistical and/or mathematical skills to better understand analytical results without having to resort to spreadsheets.

Traditional data visualization tools query data from relational databases, OLAP systems, data warehouses and spreadsheets to present both descriptive and diagnostic analytics results.

Data Visualization for Big Data

Big Data solutions require data visualization tools that can seamlessly connect to structured, semi-structured and unstructured data sources and are further capable of handling millions of data records. Data visualization tools for Big Data solutions generally use in-memory analytical technologies that reduce the latency normally attributed to traditional, disk-based data visualization tools.

Advanced data visualization tools for Big Data solutions incorporate predictive and prescriptive data analytics and data transformation features. These tools eliminate the need for data pre-processing methods, such as ETL. The tools also provide the ability to directly connect to structured, semi-structured and unstructured data sources. As part of Big Data solutions, advanced data visualization tools can join structured and unstructured data that is kept in memory for fast data access. Queries and statistical formulas can then be applied as part of various data analysis tasks for viewing data in a user-friendly format, such as on a dashboard.

Common features of visualization tools used in Big Data:

- Aggregation – provides a holistic and summarized view of data across multiple contexts
- Drill-down – enables a detailed view of the data of interest by focusing in on a data subset from the summarized view
- Filtering – helps focus on a particular set of data by filtering away the data that is not of immediate interest
- Roll-up – groups data across multiple categories to show subtotals and totals

- What-if analysis – enables multiple outcomes to be visualized by enabling related factors to be dynamically changed.

Chapter V

Big Data Storage Concepts

Data acquired from external sources is often not in a format or structure that can be directly processed. To overcome these incompatibilities and prepare data for storage and processing, data wrangling is necessary. Data wrangling includes steps to filter, cleanse and otherwise prepare the data for downstream analysis. From a storage perspective, a copy of the data is first stored in its acquired format, and, after wrangling, the prepared data needs to be stored again. Typically, storage is required whenever the following occurs:

- External datasets are acquired, or internal data will be used in a Big Data environment
- Data is manipulated to be made amenable for data analysis
- Data is processed via an ETL activity, or output is generated as a result of an analytical operation

Due to the need to store Big Data datasets, often in multiple copies, innovative storage strategies and technologies have been created to achieve cost-effective and highly scalable storage solutions. In order to understand the underlying mechanisms behind Big Data storage technology, the following topics are introduced in this chapter: Clusters, File systems and distributed files systems, NoSQL, Sharding, Replication, CAP theorem, ACID, BASE.

5.1 Clusters

In computing, a cluster is a tightly coupled collection of servers, or nodes. These servers usually have the same hardware specifications and are connected together via a network to work as a single unit, as shown in Figure 5.1. Each node in the cluster has its own dedicated resources, such as memory, a processor, and a hard drive. A cluster can execute a task by splitting it into small pieces and distributing their execution onto different computers that belong to the cluster.

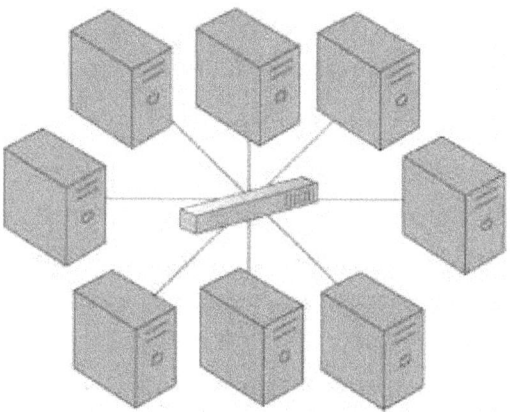

Figure 5.1 The symbol used to represent a cluster.

5.2 File Systems and Distributed File Systems

A file system is the method of storing and organizing data on a storage device, such as flash drives, DVDs and hard drives. A file is an atomic unit of storage used by the file system to store data. A file system provides a logical view of the data stored on the storage device and presents it as a tree structure of directories and files as pictured in Figure 5.2. Operating systems employ file systems to store and retrieve data on behalf of applications. Each operating system provides support for one or more file systems, for example NTFS on Microsoft Windows and ext on Linux.

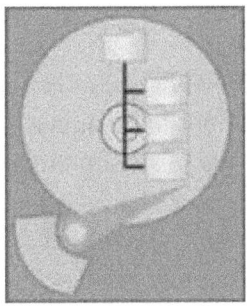

Figure 5.2 The symbol used to represent a file system.

A distributed file system is a file system that can store large files spread across the nodes of a cluster, as illustrated in Figure 5.3. To the client, files appear to be local; however, this is only a logical view as physically the files are distributed throughout the cluster. This local view is presented via the distributed file system and it enables the files to be accessed from multiple locations. Examples include the Google File System (GFS) and Hadoop Distributed File System (HDFS).

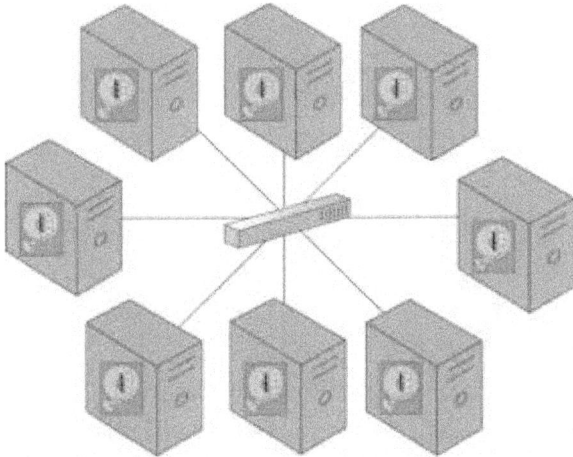

Figure 5.3 The symbol used to represent distributed file systems.

5.3 NoSQL

A Not-only SQL (NoSQL) database is a non-relational database that is highly scalable, fault-tolerant and specifically designed to house semi-structured and unstructured data. A NoSQL database often provides an API-based query interface that can be called from within an application. NoSQL databases also support query languages other than Structured Query Language (SQL) because SQL was designed to query structured data stored within a relational database. As an example, a NoSQL database that is optimized to store XML files will often use XQuery as the query language. Likewise, a NoSQL database designed to store RDF data will use SPARQL to query the relationships it contains. That being said, there are some NoSQL databases that also provide an SQL-like query interface, as shown in Figure 5.4.

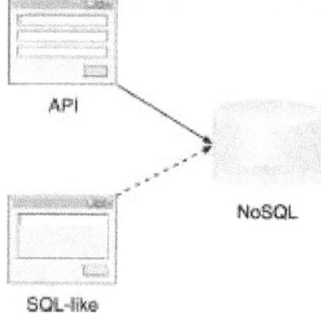

Figure 5.4 A NoSQL database can provide an API- or SQL-like query interface.

5.4 Sharding

Sharding is the process of horizontally partitioning a large dataset into a collection of smaller, more manageable datasets called shards. The shards are distributed across multiple nodes, where a node is a server or a machine (Figure 5.5). Each shard is stored on a separate node and each node is responsible for only the data stored on it. Each shard shares the same schema, and all shards collectively represent the complete dataset.

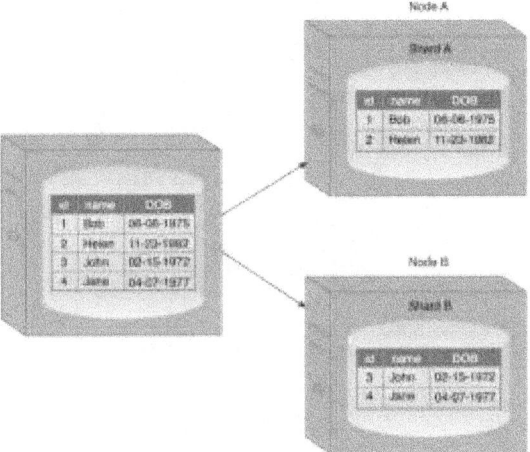

Figure 5.5 An example of sharding where a dataset is spread across Node A and Node B, resulting in Shard A and Shard B, respectively.

Sharding is often transparent to the client, but this is not a requirement. Sharding allows the distribution of processing loads across multiple nodes to achieve horizontal scalability. Horizontal scaling is a method for increasing a system's capacity by adding similar or higher capacity resources alongside existing resources. Since each node is responsible for only a part of the whole dataset, read/write times are greatly improved.

Figure 5.6 presents an illustration of how sharding works in practice:

- Each shard can independently service reads and writes for the specific subset of data that it is responsible for.
- Depending on the query, data may need to be fetched from both shards.

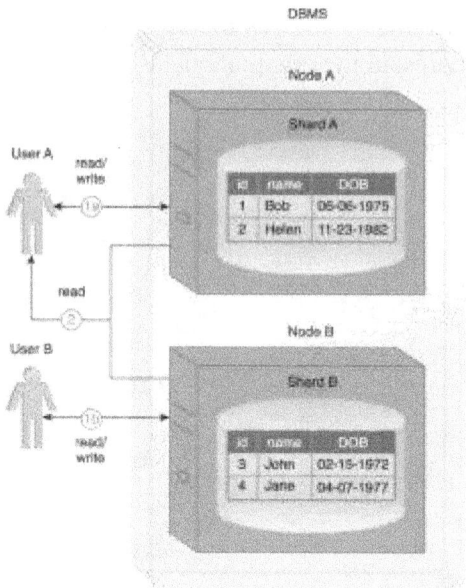

Figure 5.6 A sharding example where data is fetched from both Node A and Node B.

A benefit of sharding is that it provides partial tolerance toward failures. In case of a node failure, only data stored on that node is affected.

With regards to data partitioning, query patterns need to be taken into account so that shards themselves do not become performance bottlenecks. For example, queries requiring data from multiple shards will impose performance penalties. Data locality keeps commonly accessed data co-located on a single shard and helps counter such performance issues.

5.5 Replication

Replication stores multiple copies of a dataset, known as replicas, on multiple nodes

(Figure 5.7). Replication provides scalability and availability due to the fact that the same data is replicated on various nodes. Fault tolerance is also achieved since data redundancy ensures that data is not lost when an individual node fails. There are two different methods that are used to implement replication:

- master-slave
- peer-to-peer

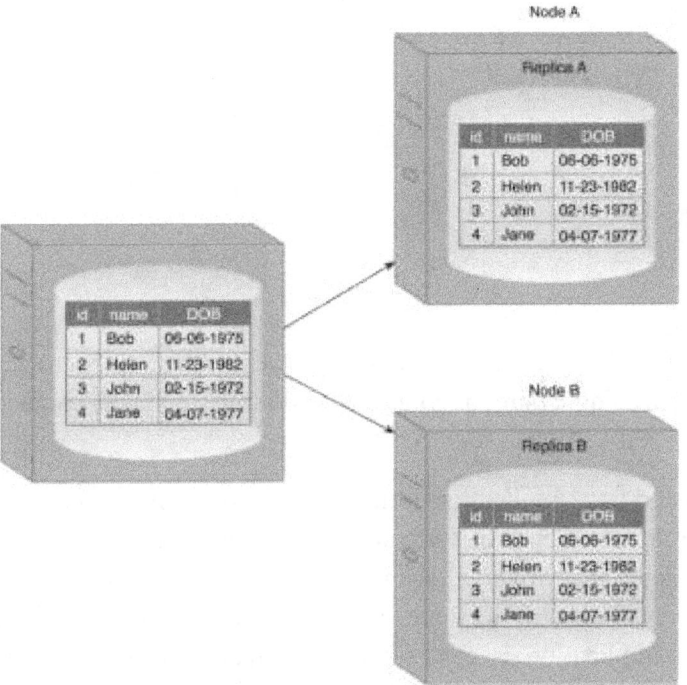

Figure 5.7 An example of replication where a dataset is replicated to Node A and Node B, resulting in Replica A and Replica B.

Master-Slave

During master-slave replication, nodes are arranged in a master-slave configuration, and all data is written to a master node. Once saved, the data is replicated over to multiple slave nodes. All external write requests, including insert, update and delete, occur on the master node, whereas read requests can be fulfilled by any slave node. In Figure 5.8, writes are managed by the master node and data can be read from either Slave A or Slave B.

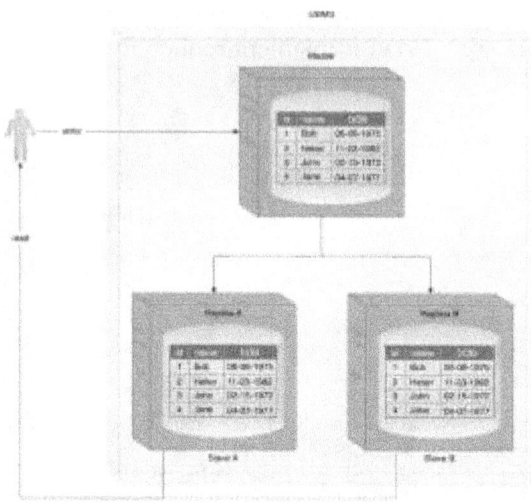

Figure 5.8 An example of master-slave replication where Master A is the single point of contact for all writes, and data can be read from Slave A and Slave B.

Master-slave replication is ideal for read intensive loads rather than write intensive loads since growing read demands can be managed by horizontal scaling to add more slave nodes. Writes are consistent, as all writes are coordinated by the master node. The implication is that write performance will suffer as the amount of writes increases. If the master node fails, reads are still possible via any of the slave nodes.

A slave node can be configured as a backup node for the master node. In the event that the master node fails, writes are not supported until a master node is reestablished. The master node is either resurrected from a backup of the master node, or a new master node is chosen from the slave nodes.

One concern with master-slave replication is read inconsistency, which can be an issue if a slave node is read prior to an update to the master being copied to it. To ensure read consistency, a voting system can be implemented where a read is declared consistent if the majority of the slaves contain the same version of the record. Implementation of such a voting system requires a reliable and fast communication mechanism between the slaves.

Figure 5.9 illustrates a scenario where read inconsistency occurs.

1. User A updates data.
2. The data is copied over to Slave A by the Master.
3. Before the data is copied over to Slave B, User B tries to read the data from Slave B, which results in an inconsistent read.
4. The data will eventually become consistent when Slave B is updated by the Master.

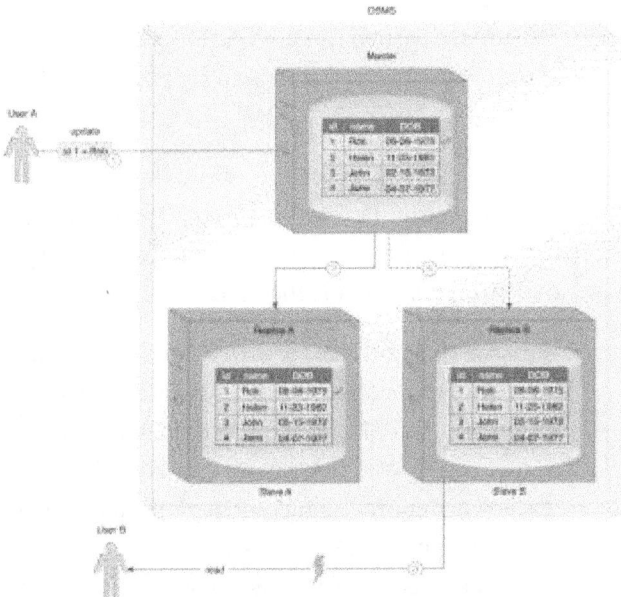

Figure 5.9 An example of master-slave replication where read inconsistency occurs.

Peer-to-Peer

With peer-to-peer replication, all nodes operate at the same level. In other words, there is not a master-slave relationship between the nodes. Each node, known as a peer, is equally capable of handling reads and writes. Each write is copied to all peers, as illustrated in Figure 5.10.

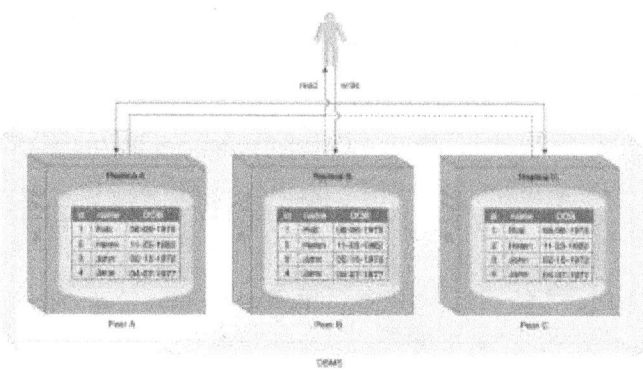

Figure 5.10 Writes are copied to Peers A, B and C simultaneously. Data is read from Peer A, but it can also be read from Peers B or C.

Peer-to-peer replication is prone to write inconsistencies that occur as a result of a simultaneous update of the same data across multiple peers. This can be addressed by implementing either a pessimistic or optimistic concurrency strategy.

- Pessimistic concurrency is a proactive strategy that prevents inconsistency. It uses locking to ensure that only one update to a record can occur at a time. However, this is detrimental to availability since the database record being updated remains unavailable until all locks are released.
- Optimistic concurrency is a reactive strategy that does not use locking. Instead, it allows inconsistency to

occur with knowledge that eventually consistency will be achieved after all updates have propagated.

With optimistic concurrency, peers may remain inconsistent for some period of time before attaining consistency. However, the database remains available as no locking is involved. Like master-slave replication, reads can be inconsistent during the time period when some of the peers have completed their updates while others perform their updates. However, reads eventually become consistent when the updates have been executed on all peers.

To ensure read consistency, a voting system can be implemented where a read is declared consistent if the majority of the peers contain the same version of the record. As previously indicated, implementation of such a voting system requires a reliable and fast communication mechanism between the peers.

Figure 5.11 demonstrates a scenario where an inconsistent read occurs.

1. User A updates data.
2. a. The data is copied over to Peer A.

b. The data is copied over to Peer B.

3. Before the data is copied over to Peer C, User B tries to read the data from Peer C, resulting in an inconsistent read.
4. The data will eventually be updated on Peer C, and the database will once again become consistent.

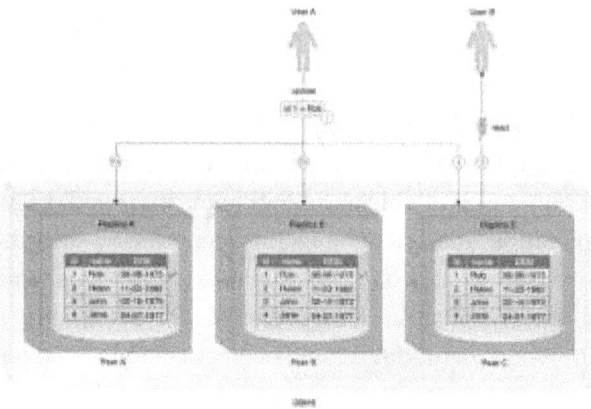

Figure 5.11 An example of peer-to-peer replication where an inconsistent read occurs.

5.6 Sharding and Replication

To improve on the limited fault tolerance offered by sharding, while additionally benefiting from the increased availability and scalability of replication, both sharding and replication can be combined, as shown in Figure 5.12.

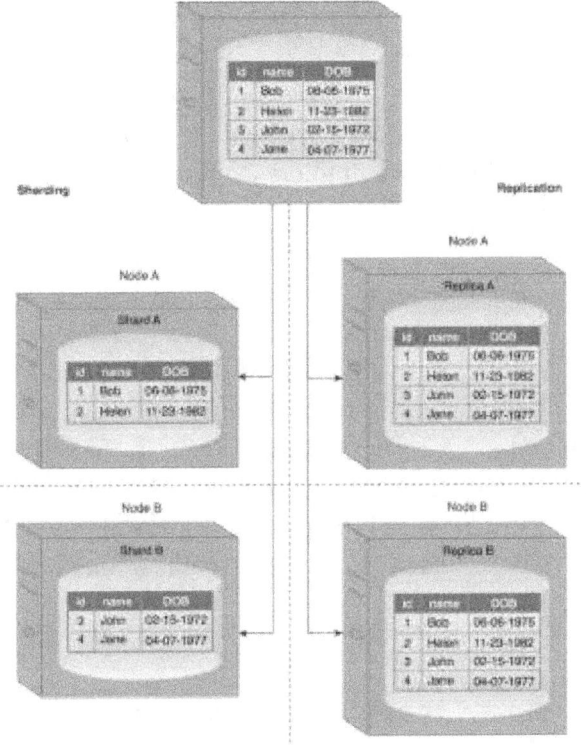

Figure 5.12 A comparison of sharding and replication that shows how a dataset is distributed between two nodes with the different approaches.

This section covers the following combinations:

- sharding and master-slave replication
- sharding and peer-to-peer replication

Combining Sharding and Master-Slave Replication

When sharding is combined with master-slave replication, multiple shards become slaves of a single master, and the master itself is a shard. Although this results in multiple masters, a single slave-shard can only be managed by a single master-shard.

Write consistency is maintained by the master-shard. However, if the master-shard becomes non-operational or a network outage occurs, fault tolerance with regards to write operations is impacted. Replicas of shards are kept on multiple slave nodes to provide scalability and fault tolerance for read operations.

In Figure 5.13:

- Each node acts both as a master and a slave for different shards.
- Writes (id = 2) to Shard A are regulated by Node A, as it is the master for Shard A.
- Node A replicates data (id = 2) to Node B, which is a slave for Shard A.
- Reads (id = 4) can be served directly by either Node B or Node C as they each contain Shard B.

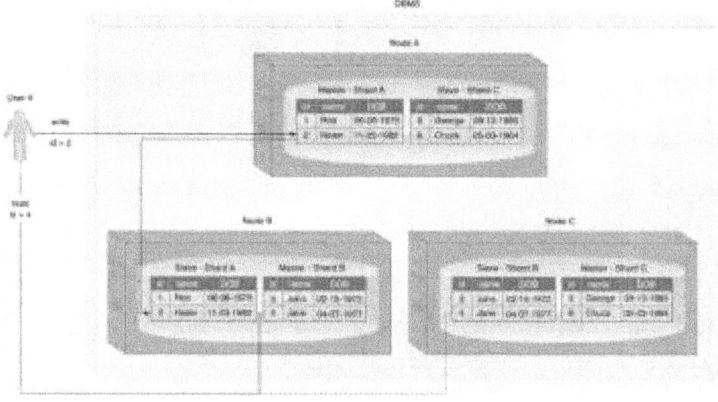

Figure 5.13 An example that shows the combination of sharding and master-slave replication.

Combining Sharding and Peer-to-Peer Replication

When combining sharding with peer-to-peer replication, each shard is replicated to multiple peers, and each peer is only responsible for a subset of the overall dataset. Collectively, this helps achieve increased scalability and fault tolerance. As there is no master involved, there is no single point of failure and fault-tolerance for both read and write operations is supported.

In Figure 5.14:

- Each node contains replicas of two different shards.
- Writes (id = 3) are replicated to both Node A and Node C (Peers) as they are responsible for Shard C.
- Reads (id = 6) can be served by either Node B or Node C as they each contain Shard B.

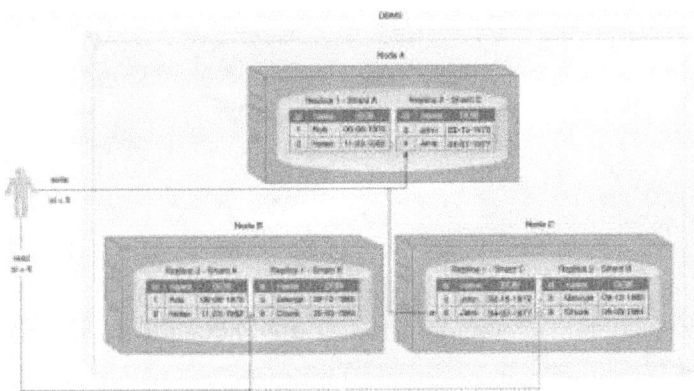

Figure 5.14 An example of the combination of sharding and peer-to-peer replication.

5.7 CAP Theorem

The Consistency, Availability, and Partition tolerance (CAP) theorem, also known as Brewer's theorem, expresses a triple constraint related to distributed database systems. It states that a distributed database system, running on a cluster, can only provide two of the following three properties:

- Consistency – A read from any node results in the same data across multiple nodes (Figure 5.15).

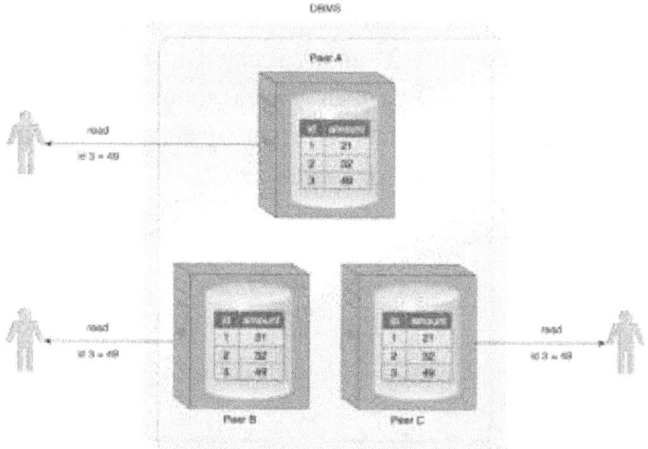

Figure 5.15 Consistency: all three users get the same value for the amount column even though three different nodes are serving the record.

- Availability – A read/write request will always be acknowledged in the form of a success or a failure (Figure 5.16).

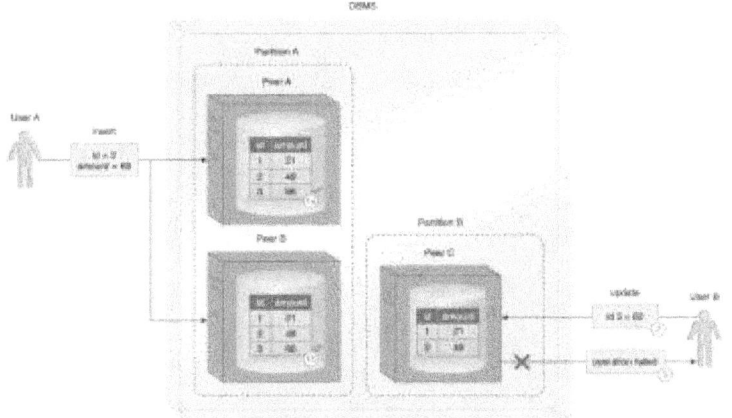

Figure 5.16 Availability and partition tolerance: in the event of a communication failure, requests from both users are still serviced (1, 2). However, with User B, the update fails as the record with id = 3 has not been copied over to Peer C. The user is duly notified (3) that the update has failed.

• Partition tolerance – The database system can tolerate communication outages that split the cluster into multiple silos and can still service read/write requests (Figure 5.16).

The following scenarios demonstrate why only two of the three properties of the CAP theorem are simultaneously supportable. To aid this discussion, Figure 5.17 provides a Venn diagram showing the areas of overlap between consistency, availability and partition tolerance.

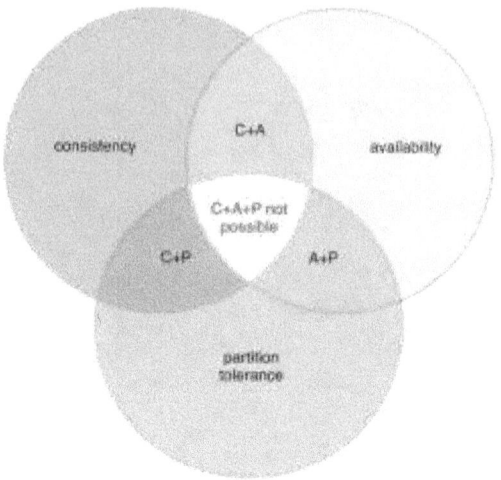

Figure 5.17 A Venn diagram summarizing the CAP theorem.

If consistency (C) and availability (A) are required, available nodes need to communicate to ensure consistency (C). Therefore, partition tolerance (P) is not possible.

If consistency (C) and partition tolerance (P) are required, nodes cannot remain available (A) as the nodes will become unavailable while achieving a state of consistency (C).

If availability (A) and partition tolerance (P) are required, then consistency (C) is not possible because of the data communication requirement between the nodes. So, the database can remain available (A) but with inconsistent results.

In a distributed database, scalability and fault tolerance can be improved through additional nodes, although this challenges consistency (C). The addition of nodes can also cause availability (A) to suffer due to the latency caused by increased communication between nodes.

Distributed database systems cannot be 100% partition tolerant (P). Although communication outages are rare and temporary, partition tolerance (P) must always be supported by a distributed database; therefore, CAP is generally a choice between choosing either C+P or A+P. The requirements of the system will dictate which is chosen.

5.8 ACID

ACID is a database design principle related to transaction management. It is an acronym that stands for:

- atomicity
- consistency
- isolation
- durability

ACID is a transaction management style that leverages pessimistic concurrency controls to ensure consistency is maintained through the application of record locks. ACID is the traditional approach to database transaction management as it is leveraged by relational database management systems.

Atomicity ensures that all operations will always succeed or fail completely. In other words, there are no partial transactions.

The following steps are illustrated in Figure 5.18:

1. A user attempts to update three records as a part of a transaction.
2. Two records are successfully updated before the occurrence of an error.
3. As a result, the database roll backs any partial effects of the transaction and puts the system back to its prior state.

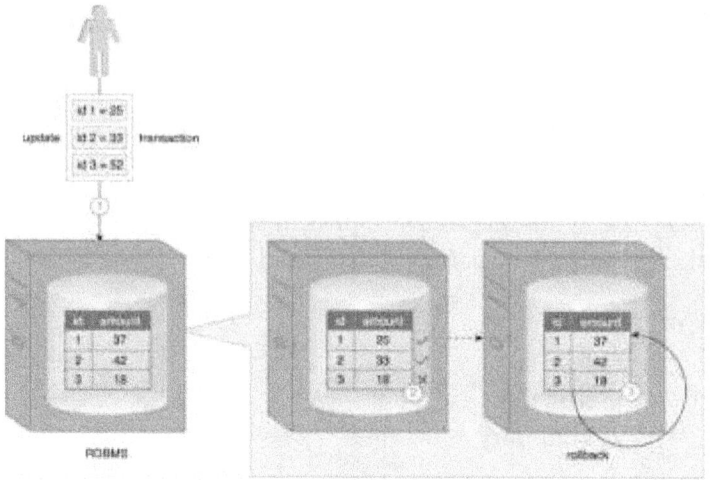

Figure 5.18 An example of the atomicity property of ACID is evident here.

Consistency ensures that the database will always remain in a consistent state by ensuring that only data that conforms to the constraints of the database schema can be written to the database. Thus a database that is in a consistent state will remain in a consistent state following a successful transaction.

In Figure 5.19:

1. A user attempts to update the amount column of the table that is of type float with a varchar value.
2. The database applies its validation check and rejects this update because the value violates the constraint checks for the amount column.

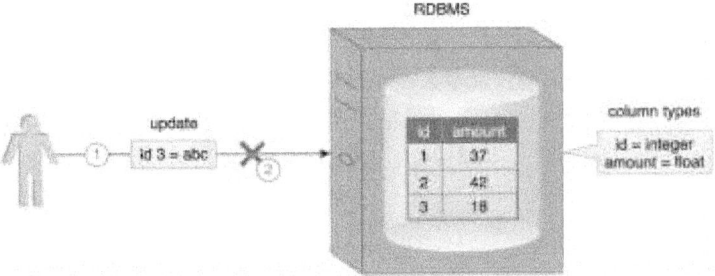

Figure 5.19 An example of the consistency of ACID.

Isolation ensures that the results of a transaction are not visible to other operations until it is complete.

In Figure 5.20:

1. User A attempts to update two records as part of a transaction.
2. The database successfully updates the first record.
3. However, before it can update the second record, User B attempts to update the same record. The database does not permit User B's update until User A's update succeeds or fails in full. This occurs because the record with id3 is locked by the database until the transaction is complete.

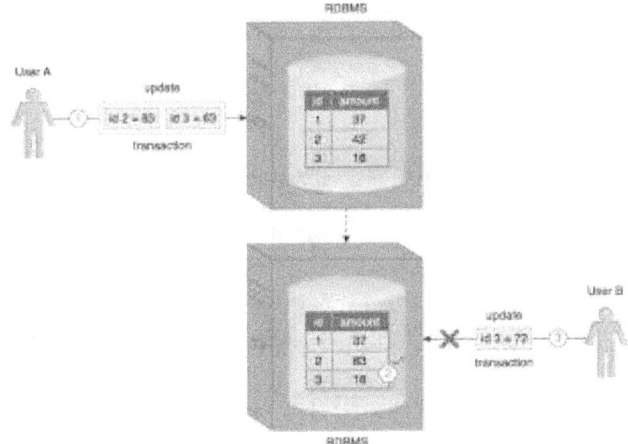

Figure 5.20 An example of the isolation property of ACID.

Durability ensures that the results of an operation are permanent. In other words, once a transaction has been committed, it cannot be rolled back. This is irrespective of any system failure.

In Figure 5.21:

1. A user updates a record as part of a transaction.
2. The database successfully updates the record.
3. Right after this update, a power failure occurs. The database maintains its state while there is no power.
4. The power is resumed.
5. The database serves the record as per last update when requested by the user.

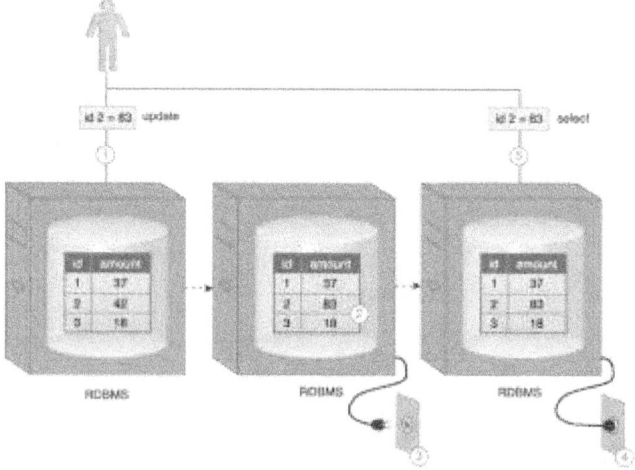

Figure 5.21 The durability characteristic of ACID.

Figure 5.22 shows the results of the application of the ACID principle:

1. User A attempts to update a record as part of a transaction.

2. The database validates the value and the update is successfully applied.

3. After the successful completion of the transaction, when Users B and C request the same record, the database provides the updated value to both the users.

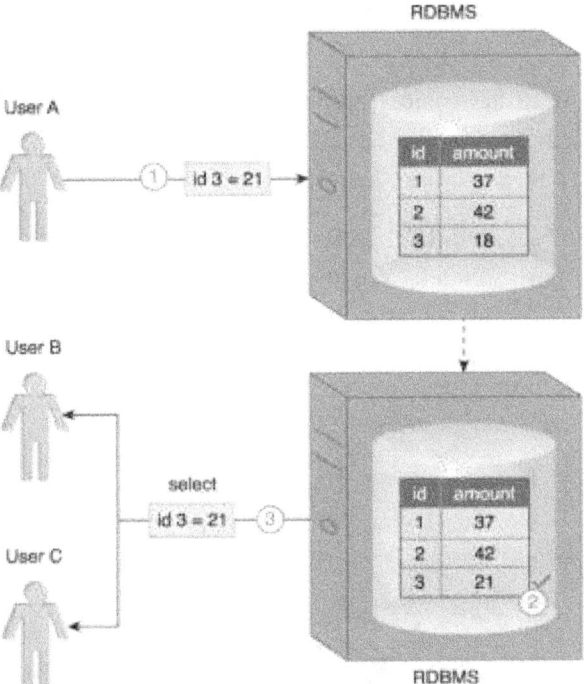

Figure 5.22 The ACID principle results in consistent database behavior.

5.9 BASE

BASE is a database design principle based on the CAP theorem and leveraged by database systems that use distributed technology. BASE stands for:

- basically available
- soft state
- eventual consistency

When a database supports BASE, it favors availability over consistency. In other words, the database is A+P from a CAP perspective. In essence, BASE leverages optimistic concurrency by relaxing the strong consistency constraints mandated by the ACID properties.

If a database is "basically available," that database will always acknowledge a client's request, either in the form of the requested data or a success/failure notification.

In Figure 5.23, the database is basically available, even though it has been partitioned as a result of a network failure.

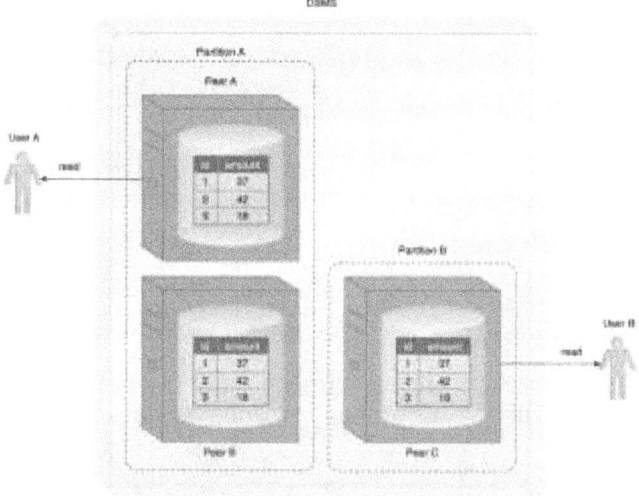

Figure 5.23 User A and User B receive data despite the database being partitioned by a network failure.

Soft state means that a database may be in an inconsistent state when data is read; thus, the results may change if the same data is requested again. This is because the data could be updated for consistency, even though no user has written to the database between the two reads. This property is closely related to eventual consistency.

In Figure 5.24:

1. User A updates a record on Peer A.
2. Before the other peers are updated, User B requests the same record from Peer C.
3. The database is now in a soft state, and stale data is returned to User B.

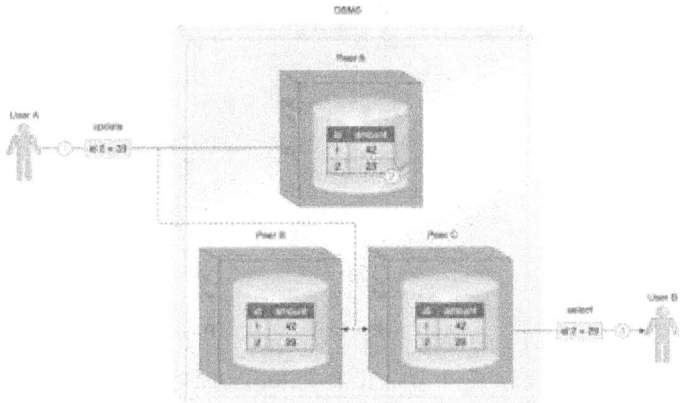

Figure 5.24 An example of the soft state property of BASE is shown here.

Eventual consistency is the state in which reads by different clients, immediately following a write to the database, may not return consistent results. The database only attains consistency once the changes have been propagated to all nodes. While the database is in the process of attaining the state of eventual consistency, it will be in a soft state.

In Figure 5.25:

1. User A updates a record.
2. The record only gets updated at Peer A, but before the other peers can be updated, User B requests the same record.

3. The database is now in a soft state. Stale data is returned to User B from Peer C.
4. However, the consistency is eventually attained, and User C gets the correct value.

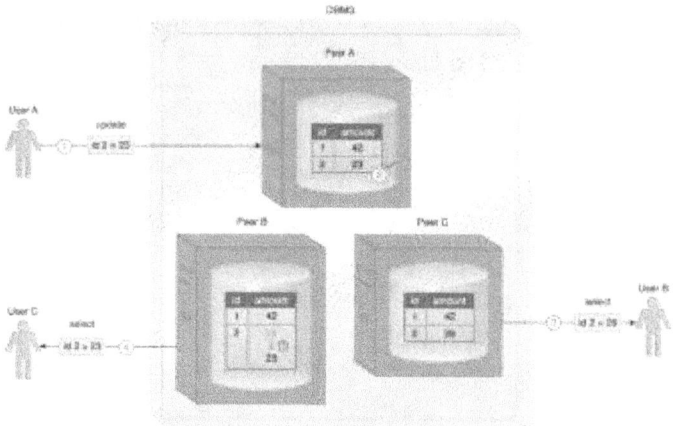

Figure 5.25 An example of the eventual consistency property of BASE.

BASE emphasizes availability over immediate consistency, in contrast to ACID, which ensures immediate consistency at the expense of availability due to record locking. This soft approach toward consistency allows BASE compliant databases to serve multiple clients without any latency albeit serving inconsistent results. However, BASE-compliant databases are not useful for transactional systems where lack of consistency is a concern.

Chapter VI

Big Data Processing Concepts

The need to process large volumes of data is not new. When considering the relationship between a data warehouse and its associated data marts, it becomes clear that partitioning a large dataset into a smaller one can speed up processing. Big Data datasets stored on distributed file systems or within a distributed database are already partitioned into smaller datasets. The key to understanding Big Data processing is the realization that unlike the centralized processing, which occurs within a traditional relational database, Big Data is often processed in parallel in a distributed fashion at the location in which it is stored.

Of course, not all Big Data is batch-processed. Some data possesses the velocity characteristic and arrives in a time-ordered stream. Big Data analytics has answers for this type of processing as well. By leveraging in-memory storage architectures, sense-making can occur to deliver situational awareness. An important principle that constrains streaming Big Data processing is called the Speed, Consistency, and Volume (SCV) principle. It is detailed within this chapter as well.

To further the discussion of Big Data processing, each of the following concepts will be examined in turn:

- Parallel data processing
- Distributed data processing
- Hadoop
- Processing workloads
- Cluster

6.1 Parallel Data Processing

Parallel data processing involves the simultaneous execution of multiple sub-tasks that collectively comprise a larger task. The goal is to reduce the execution time by dividing a single larger task into multiple smaller tasks that run concurrently.

Although parallel data processing can be achieved through multiple networked machines, it is more typically achieved within the confines of a single machine with multiple processors or cores, as shown in Figure 6.1.

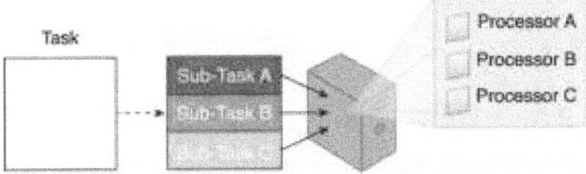

Figure 6.1 A task can be divided into three sub-tasks that are executed in parallel on three different processors within the same machine.

6.2 Distributed Data Processing

Distributed data processing is closely related to parallel data processing in that the same principle of "divide-and-conquer" is applied. However, distributed data processing is always achieved through physically separate machines that are networked together as a cluster. In Figure 6.2, a task is divided into three sub-tasks that are then executed on three different machines sharing one physical switch.

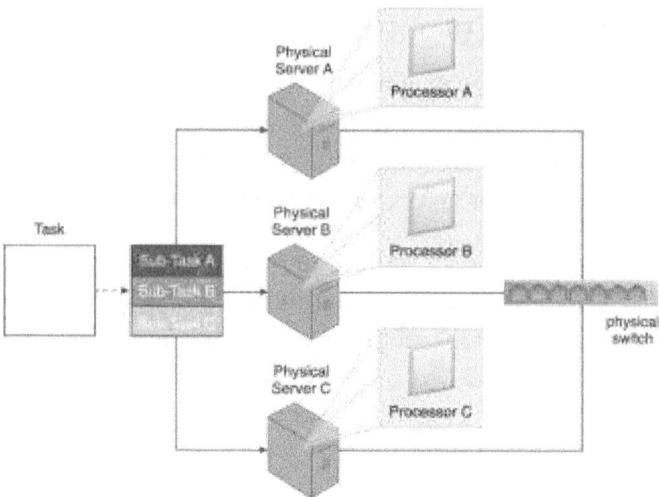

Figure 6.2 An example of distributed data processing.

6.3 Hadoop

Hadoop is an open-source framework for large-scale data storage and data processing that is compatible with commodity hardware. The Hadoop framework has established itself as a de facto industry platform for contemporary Big Data solutions. It can be used as an ETL engine or as an analytics engine for processing large amounts of structured, semi-structured and unstructured data. From an analysis perspective, Hadoop implements the MapReduce processing framework. Figure 6.3 illustrates some of Hadoop's features.

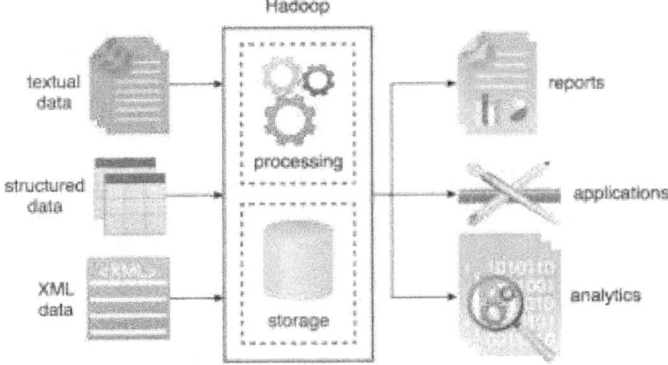

Figure 6.3 Hadoop is a versatile framework that provides both processing and storage capabilities.

6.4 Processing Workloads

A processing workload in Big Data is defined as the amount and nature of data that is processed within a certain amount of time. Workloads are usually divided into two types:

- batch
- transactional

Batch

Batch processing, also known as offline processing, involves processing data in batches and usually imposes delays, which in turn results in high-latency responses. Batch workloads typically involve large quantities of data with sequential read/writes and comprise of groups of read or write queries.

Queries can be complex and involve multiple joins. OLAP systems commonly process workloads in batches. Strategic BI and analytics are batch-oriented as they are highly read-intensive tasks involving large volumes of data. As shown in Figure 6.4, a batch workload comprises grouped read/writes that have a large data footprint and may contain complex joins and provide high-latency responses.

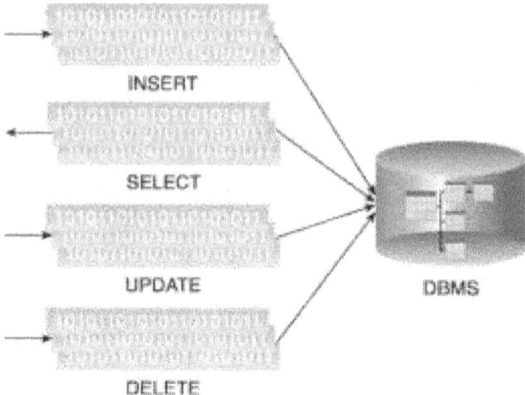

Figure 6.4 A batch workload can include grouped read/writes to INSERT, SELECT, UPDATE and DELETE.

Transactional

Transactional processing is also known as online processing. Transactional workload processing follows an approach whereby data is processed interactively without delay, resulting in low-latency responses. Transaction workloads involve small amounts of data with random reads and writes.

OLTP and operational systems, which are generally write-intensive, fall within this category. Although these workloads contain a mix of read/write queries, they are generally more write-intensive than read-intensive.

Transactional workloads comprise random reads/writes that involve fewer joins than business intelligence and reporting workloads. Given their online nature and operational significance to the enterprise, they require low-latency responses with a smaller data footprint, as shown in Figure 6.5.

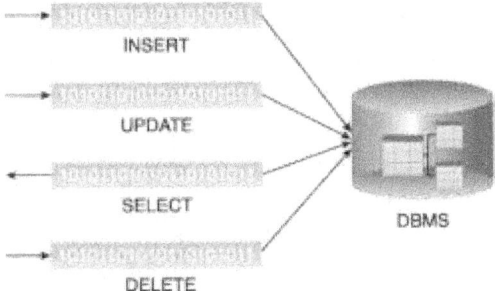

Figure 6.5 Transactional workloads have few joins and lower latency responses than batch workloads.

6.5 Cluster

In the same manner that clusters provide necessary support to create horizontally scalable storage solutions, clusters also provides the mechanism to enable distributed data processing with linear scalability. Since clusters are highly scalable, they provide an ideal environment for Big Data processing as large datasets can be divided into smaller datasets and then processed in parallel in a distributed manner. When leveraging a cluster, Big Data datasets can either be processed in batch mode or realtime mode (Figure 6.6). Ideally, a cluster will be comprised of low-cost commodity nodes that collectively provide increased processing capacity.

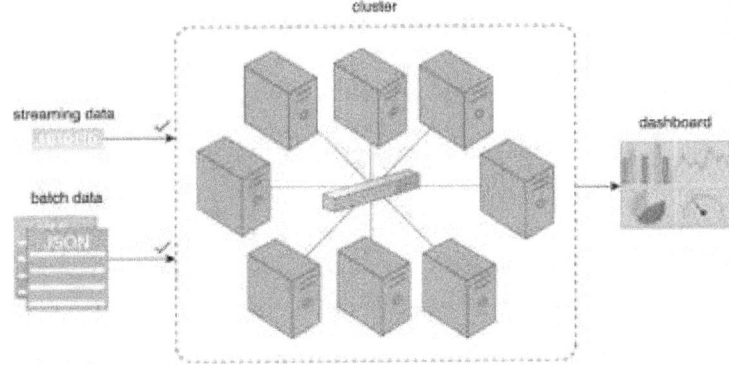

Figure 6.6 A cluster can be utilized to support batch processing of bulk data and realtime processing of streaming data.

An additional benefit of clusters is that they provide inherent redundancy and fault tolerance, as they consist of physically separate nodes. Redundancy and fault tolerance allow resilient processing and analysis to occur if a network or node failure occurs. Due to fluctuations in the processing demands placed upon a Big Data environment, leveraging cloud-host infrastructure services, or ready-made analytical environments as the backbone of a cluster, is sensible due to their elasticity and pay-for-use model of utility-based computing.

6.6 Processing in Batch Mode

In batch mode, data is processed offline in batches and the response time could vary from minutes to hours. As well, data must be persisted to the disk before it can be processed. Batch mode generally involves processing a range of large datasets, either on their own or joined together, essentially addressing the volume and variety characteristics of Big Data datasets.

The majority of Big Data processing occurs in batch mode. It is relatively simple, easy to set up and low in cost compared to realtime mode. Strategic BI, predictive and prescriptive analytics and ETL operations are commonly batch-oriented.

Batch Processing with MapReduce

MapReduce is a widely used implementation of a batch processing framework. It is highly scalable and reliable and is based on the principle of divide-and-conquer, which provides built-in fault tolerance and redundancy. It divides a big problem into a collection of smaller problems that can each be solved quickly. MapReduce has roots in both distributed and parallel computing. MapReduce is a batch-oriented processing engine (Figure 6.7) used to process large datasets using parallel processing deployed over clusters of commodity hardware.

Figure 6.7 The symbol used to represent a processing engine.

MapReduce does not require that the input data conform to any particular data model. Therefore, it can be used to process schema-less datasets. A dataset is broken down into multiple smaller parts, and operations are performed on each part independently and in parallel. The results from all operations are then summarized to arrive at the answer. Because of the coordination overhead involved in managing a job, the MapReduce processing engine generally only supports batch workloads as this work is not expected to have low latency. MapReduce is based on Google's research paper on the subject, published in early 2000.

The MapReduce processing engine works differently compared to the traditional data processing paradigm. Traditionally, data processing requires moving data from the storage node to the processing node that runs the data processing algorithm. This approach works fine for smaller datasets; however, with large datasets, moving data can incur more overhead than the actual processing of the data.

With MapReduce, the data processing algorithm is instead moved to the nodes that store the data. The data processing algorithm executes in parallel on these nodes, thereby eliminating the need to move the data first. This not only saves network bandwidth but it also results in a large reduction in processing time for large datasets, since processing smaller chunks of data in parallel is much faster.

Map and Reduce Tasks

A single processing run of the MapReduce processing engine is known as a MapReduce job. Each MapReduce job is composed of a map task and a reduce task and each task consists of multiple stages. Figure 6.8 shows the map and reduce task, along with their individual stages.

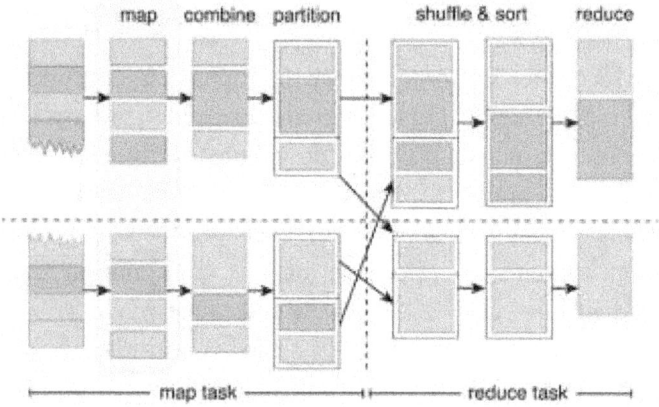

Figure 6.8 An illustration of a MapReduce job with the map stage highlighted. Map tasks

- map
- combine (optional)
- partition
- shuffle and sort
- reduce

Map

The first stage of MapReduce is known as map, during which the dataset file is divided into multiple smaller splits. Each split is parsed into its constituent records as a key-value pair. The key is usually the ordinal position of the record, and the value is the actual record.

The parsed key-value pairs for each split are then sent to a map function or mapper, with one mapper function per split. The map function executes user-defined logic. Each split generally contains multiple key-value pairs, and the mapper is run once for each key-value pair in the split.

The mapper processes each key-value pair as per the user-defined logic and further generates a key-value pair as its output. The output key can either be the same as the input key or a substring value from the input value, or another serializable user-defined object. Similarly, the output value can either be the same as the input value or a substring value from the input value, or another serializable user-defined object.

When all records of the split have been processed, the output is a list of key-value pairs where multiple key-value pairs can exist for the same key. It should be noted that for an input key-value pair, a mapper may not produce any output key-value pair (filtering) or can generate multiple key-value pairs (demultiplexing.) The map stage can be summarized by the equation shown in Figure 6.9.

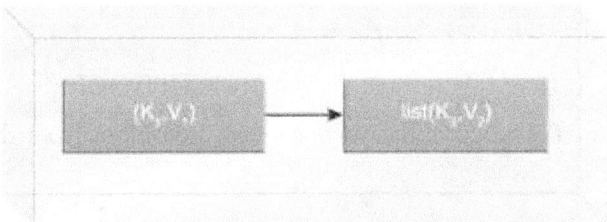

Figure 6.9 A summary of the map stage.

Combine

Generally, the output of the map function is handled directly by the reduce function. However, map tasks and reduce tasks are mostly run over different nodes. This requires moving data between mappers and reducers. This data movement can consume a lot of valuable bandwidth and directly contributes to processing latency.

With larger datasets, the time taken to move the data between map and reduce stages can exceed the actual processing undertaken by the map and reduce tasks. For this reason, the MapReduce engine provides an optional combine function (combiner) that summarizes a mapper's output before it gets processed by the reducer. Figure 6.10 illustrates the consolidation of the output from the map stage by the combine stage.

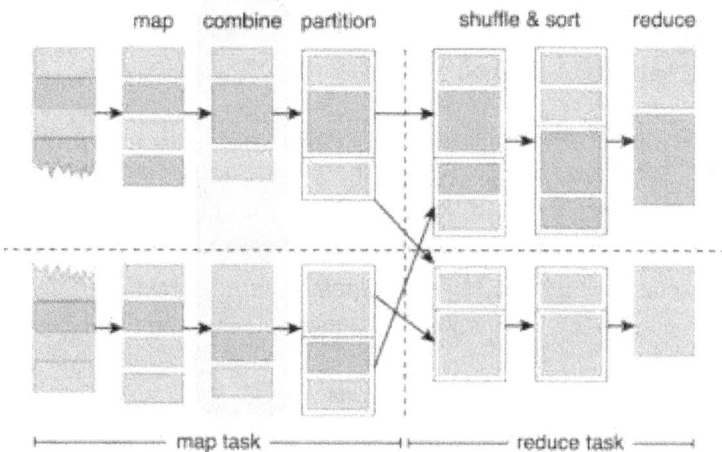

Figure 6.10 The combine stage groups the output from the map stage.

A combiner is essentially a reducer function that locally groups a mapper's output on the same node as the mapper. A reducer function can be used as a combiner function, or a custom user-defined function can be used.

The MapReduce engine combines all values for a given key from the mapper output, creating multiple key-value pairs as input to the combiner where the key is not repeated and the value exists as a list of all corresponding values for that key. The combiner stage is only an optimization stage, and may therefore not even be called by the MapReduce engine.

For example, a combiner function will work for finding the largest or the smallest number, but will not work for finding the average of all numbers since it only works with a subset of the data. The combine stage can be summarized by the equation shown in Figure 6.11.

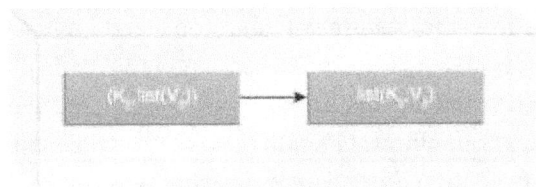

Figure 6.11 A summary of the combine stage.

Partition

During the partition stage, if more than one reducer is involved, a partitioner divides the output from the mapper or combiner (if specified and called by the MapReduce engine) into partitions between reducer instances. The number of partitions will equal the number of reducers. Figure 6.12 shows the partition stage assigning the outputs from the combine stage to specific reducers.

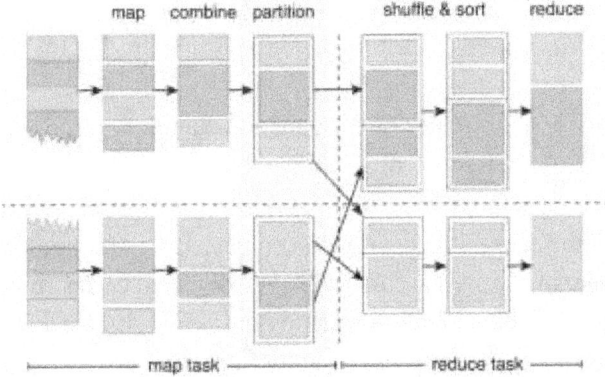

Figure 6.12 The partition stage assigns output from the map task to reducers.

Although each partition contains multiple key-value pairs, all records for a particular key are assigned to the same partition. The MapReduce engine guarantees a random and fair distribution between reducers while making sure that all of the same keys across multiple mappers end up with the same reducer instance.

Depending on the nature of the job, certain reducers can sometimes receive a large number of key-value pairs compared to others. As a result of this uneven workload, some reducers will finish earlier than others. Overall, this is less efficient and leads to longer job execution times than if the work was evenly split across reducers. This can be rectified by customizing the partitioning logic in order to guarantee a fair distribution of key-value pairs.

The partition function is the last stage of the map task. It returns the index of the reducer to which a particular partition should be sent. The partition stage can be summarized by the equation in Figure 6.13.

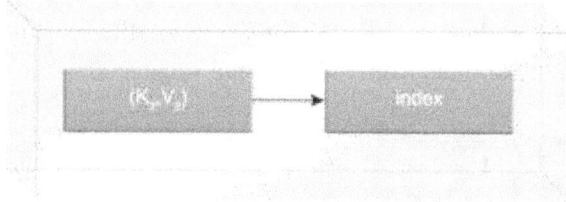

Figure 6.13 A summary of the partition stage.

Shuffle and Sort

During the first stage of the reduce task, output from all partitioners is copied across the network to the nodes running the reduce task. This is known as shuffling. The list based key-value output from each partitioner can contain the same key multiple times.

Next, the MapReduce engine automatically groups and sorts the key-value pairs according to the keys so that the output contains a sorted list of all input keys and their values with the same keys appearing together. The way in which keys are grouped and sorted can be customized.

This merge creates a single key-value pair per group, where key is the group key and the value is the list of all group values. This stage can be summarized by the equation in Figure 6.14.

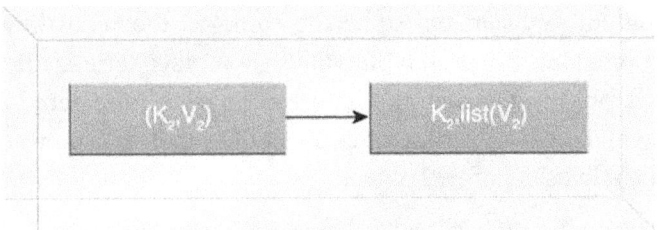

Figure 6.14 A summary of the shuffle and sort stage.

Figure 6.15 depicts a hypothetical MapReduce job that is executing the shuffle and sort stage of the reduce task.

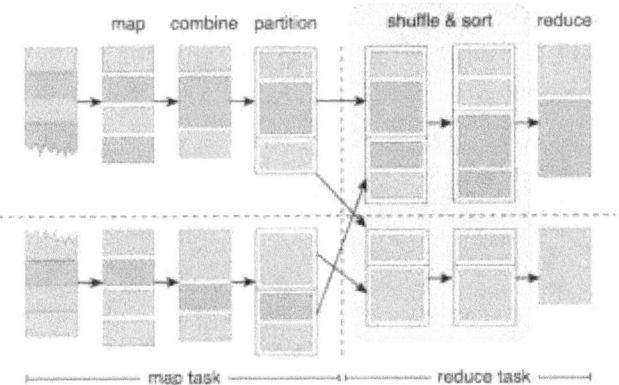

Figure 6.15 During the shuffle and sort stage, data is copied across the network to the reducer nodes and sorted by key.

Reduce

Reduce is the final stage of the reduce task. Depending on the user-defined logic specified in the reduce function (reducer), the reducer will either further summarize its input or will emit the output without making any changes. In either case, for each key-value pair that a reducer receives, the list of values stored in the value part of the pair is processed and another key-value pair is written out.

The output key can either be the same as the input key or a substring value from the input value, or another serializable user-defined object. The output value can either be the same as the input value or a substring value from the input value, or another serializable user-defined object.

Note that just like the mapper, for the input key-value pair, a reducer may not produce any output key-value pair (filtering) or can generate multiple key-value pairs (demultiplexing). The output of the reducer, that is the key-value pairs, is then written out as a separate file —one file per reducer. This is depicted in Figure 6.16, which highlights the reduce stage of the reduce task. To view the full output from the MapReduce job, all the file parts must be combined.

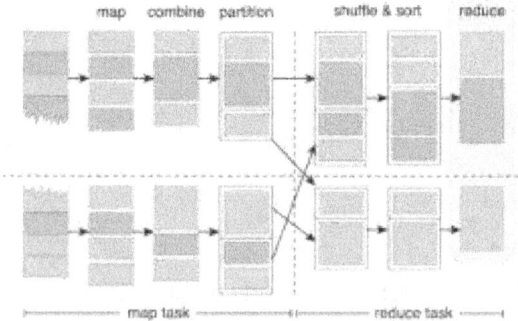

Figure 6.16 The reduce stage is the last stage of the reduce task.

The number of reducers can be customized. It is also possible to have a MapReduce job without a reducer, for example when performing filtering.

Note that the output signature (key-value types) of the map function should match that of the input signature (key-value types) of the reduce/combine function. The reduce stage can be summarized by the equation in Figure 6.17.

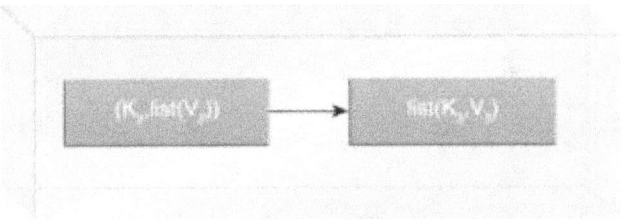

Figure 6.17 A summary of the reduce stage.

A Simple MapReduce Example

The following steps are shown in Figure 6.18:

1. The input (sales.txt) is divided into two splits.
2. Two map tasks running on two different nodes, Node A and Node B, extract product and quantity from the respective split's records in parallel. The output from each map function is a key-value pair where product is the key while quantity is the value.
3. The combiner then performs local summation of product quantities.
4. As there is only one reduce task, no partitioning is performed.
5. The output from the two map tasks is then copied to a third node, Node C, that runs the shuffle stage as part of the reduce task.
6. The sort stage then groups all quantities of the same product together as a list.

7. Like the combiner, the reduce function then sums up the quantities of each unique product in order to create the output.

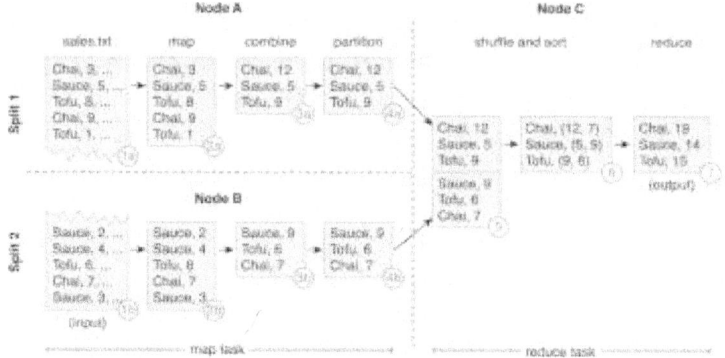

Figure 6.18 An example of MapReduce in action.

Understanding MapReduce Algorithms

Unlike traditional programming models, MapReduce follows a distinct programming model. In order to understand how algorithms can be designed or adapted to this programming model, its design principle first needs to be explored.

As described earlier, MapReduce works on the principle of divide-and-conquer. However, it is important to understand the semantics of this principle in the context of MapReduce. The divide-and-conquer principle is generally achieved using one of the following approaches:

• Task Parallelism – Task parallelism refers to the parallelization of data processing by dividing a task into sub-tasks and running each sub-task on a separate processor, generally on a separate node in a cluster (Figure 6.19). Each sub-task generally executes a different algorithm, with its own copy of the same data or different data as its input, in parallel. Generally, the output from multiple sub-tasks is joined together to obtain the final set of results.

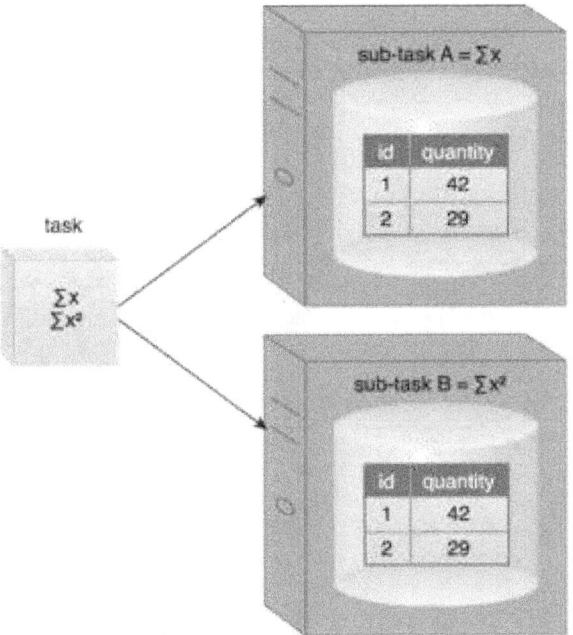

Figure 6.19 A task is split into two sub-tasks, Sub-task A and Sub-task B, which are then run on two different nodes on the same dataset.

- Data Parallelism – Data parallelism refers to the parallelization of data processing by dividing a dataset into multiple datasets and processing each sub-dataset in parallel (Figure 6.20). The sub-datasets are spread across multiple nodes and are all processed using the same algorithm. Generally, the output from each processed sub-dataset is joined together to obtain the final set of results.

Figure 6.20 A dataset is divided into two sub-datasets, Sub-dataset A and Sub-dataset B, which are then processed on two different nodes using the same function.

Within Big Data environments, the same task generally needs to be performed repeatedly on a data unit, such as a record, where the complete dataset is distributed across multiple locations due to its large size. MapReduce addresses this requirement by employing the data parallelism approach, where the data is divided into splits. Each split is then processed by its own instance of the map function, which contains the same processing logic as the other map functions.

The majority of traditional algorithmic development follows a sequential approach where operations on data are performed one after the other in such a way that subsequent operation is dependent on its preceding operation.

In MapReduce, operations are divided among the map and reduce functions. Map and reduce tasks are independent and in turn run isolated from one another. Furthermore, each instance of a map or reduce function runs independently of other instances.

Function signatures in traditional algorithmic development are generally not constrained. In MapReduce, the map and reduce function signatures are constrained to a set of key-value pairs. This is the only way that a map function can communicate with a reduce function. Apart from this, the logic in the map function is dependent on how records are parsed, which further depends on what constitutes a logical data unit within the dataset.

For example, each line in a text file generally represents a single record. However, it may be that a set of two or more lines actually constitute a single record (Figure 6.21). Furthermore, the logic within the reduce function is dependent on the output of the map function, particularly which keys were emitted from the map function as the reduce function receives a unique key with a consolidated list of all of its values. It should be noted that in some scenarios, such as with text extraction, a reduce function may not be required.

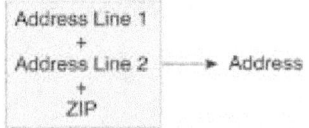

Figure 6.21 An instance where three lines constitute a single record.

The key considerations when developing a MapReduce algorithm can be summarized as follows:

- Use of relatively simplistic algorithmic logic, such that the required result can be obtained by applying the same logic to different portions of a dataset in parallel and then aggregating the results in some manner.
- Availability of the dataset in a distributed manner partitioned across a cluster so that multiple map functions can process different subsets of a dataset in parallel.
- Understanding of the data structure within the dataset so that a meaningful data unit (a single record) can be chosen.
- Dividing algorithmic logic into map and reduce functions so that the logic in the map function is not dependent on the complete dataset, since only data within a single split is available.
- Emitting the correct key from the map function along with all the required data as value because the reduce function's logic can only process those values that were emitted as part of the key-value pairs from the map function.
- Emitting the correct key from the reduce function along with the required data as value because the output from each reduce function becomes the final output of the MapReduce algorithm.

6.7 Processing in Realtime Mode

In realtime mode, data is processed in-memory as it is captured before being persisted to the disk. Response time generally ranges from a sub-second to under a minute. Realtime mode addresses the velocity characteristic of Big Data datasets.

Within Big Data processing, realtime processing is also called event or stream processing as the data either arrives continuously (stream) or at intervals (event). The individual event/stream datum is generally small in size, but its continuous nature results in very large datasets.

Another related term, interactive mode, falls within the category of realtime. Interactive mode generally refers to query processing in realtime. Operational BI/analytics are generally conducted in realtime mode.

A fundamental principle related to Big Data processing is called the Speed, Consistency and Volume (SCV) principle. It is covered first as it establishes some basic constraints on processing that mainly impact realtime processing mode.

Speed Consistency Volume (SCV)

Whereas the CAP theorem is primarily related to distributed data storage, the SCV (Figure 6.22) principle is related to distributed data processing. It states that a distributed data processing system can be designed to support only two of the following three requirements:

- Speed – Speed refers to how quickly the data can be processed once it is generated. In the case of realtime analytics, data is processed comparatively faster than batch analytics. This generally excludes the time taken to capture data and focuses only on the actual

data processing, such as generating statistics or executing an algorithm.
- Consistency – Consistency refers to the accuracy and the precision of the results. Results are deemed accurate if they are close to the correct value and precise if close to each other. A more consistent system will make use of all available data, resulting in high accuracy and precision as compared to a less consistent system that makes use of sampling techniques, which can result in lower accuracy with an acceptable level of precision.
- Volume – Volume refers to the amount of data that can be processed. Big Data's velocity characteristic results in fast growing datasets leading to huge volumes of data that need to be processed in a distributed manner. Processing such voluminous data in its entirety while ensuring speed and consistency is not possible.

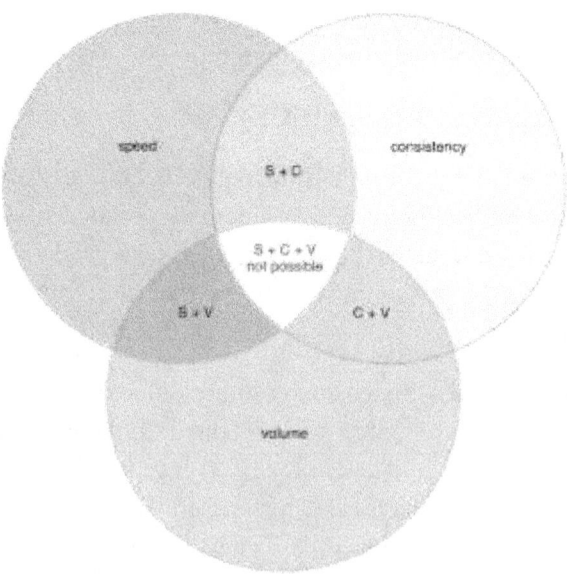

Figure 6.22 This Venn diagram summarizes the SCV principle.

If speed (S) and consistency (C) are required, it is not possible to process high volumes of data (V) because large amounts of data slow down data processing.

If consistency (C) and processing of high volumes of data (V) are required, it is not possible to process the data at high speed (S) as achieving high speed data processing requires smaller data volumes.

If high volume (V) data processing coupled with high speed (S) data processing is required, the processed results will not be consistent (C) since high-speed processing of large amounts of data involves sampling the data, which may reduce consistency.

It should be noted that the choice of which two of the three dimensions to support is fully dependent upon the system requirements of the analysis environment.

In Big Data environments, making the maximum amount of data available is mandatory for performing in-depth analysis, such as pattern identification. Hence, forgoing volume (V) over speed (S) and consistency (C) needs to be considered carefully as data may still be required for batch processing in order to glean further insights.

n the case of Big Data processing, assuming that data (V) loss is unacceptable, generally a realtime data analysis system will either be S+V or C+V, depending upon whether speed (S) or consistent results (C) is favored.

Processing Big Data in realtime generally refers to realtime or near-realtime analytics. Data is processed as it arrives at the enterprise boundary without an unreasonable delay. Instead of initially persisting the data to the disk, for example to a database, the data is first processed in memory and then persisted to the disk for future use or archival purposes. This is opposite of batch processing mode, where data is persisted to the disk first and then subsequently processed, which can create significant delays.

Analyzing Big Data in realtime requires the use of in-memory storage devices (IMDGs or IMDBs). Once in memory, the data can then be processed in realtime without incurring any hard-disk I/O latency. The realtime processing may involve calculating simple statistics, executing complex algorithms or updating the state of the in-memory data as a result of a change detected in some metric.

For enhanced data analysis, in-memory data can be combined with previously batch-processed data or denormalized data loaded from on-disk storage devices. This helps to achieve realtime data processing as datasets can be joined in memory.

Although realtime Big Data processing generally refers to incoming new data, it can also include performing queries on previously persisted data that requires interactive response. Once the data has been processed, the processing results can then be published for interested consumers. This may occur via a realtime dashboard application or a Web application that delivers realtime updates to the user.

Depending on system requirements, the processed data along with the raw input data can be offloaded to on-disk storage for subsequent complex, batch data analyses.

The following steps are shown in Figure 6.23:

1. Streaming data is captured via a data transfer engine.
2. It is then simultaneously saved to an in-memory storage device (a) and an on-disk storage device (b).
3. A processing engine is then used to process data in realtime.
4. Finally, the results are fed to a dashboard for operational analysis.

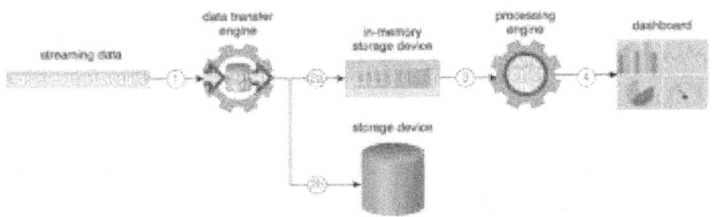

Figure 6.23 An example of realtime data processing in a Big Data environment.

Two important concepts related to realtime Big Data processing are:

- Event Stream Processing (ESP)
- Complex Event Processing (CEP)

Event Stream Processing

During ESP, an incoming stream of events, generally from a single source and ordered by time, is continuously analyzed. The analysis can occur via simple queries or the application of algorithms that are mostly formula-based. The analysis takes place in-memory before storing the events to an on-disk storage device.

Other (memory resident) data sources can also be incorporated into the analysis for performing richer analytics. The processing results can be fed to a dashboard or can act as a trigger for another application to perform a preconfigured action or further analysis. ESP focuses more on speed than complexity; the operation to be executed is comparatively simple to aid faster execution.

Complex Event Processing

During CEP, a number of realtime events often coming from disparate sources and arriving at different time intervals are analyzed simultaneously for the detection of patterns and initiation of action. Rule-based algorithms and statistical techniques are applied, taking into account business logic and process context to discover cross-cutting complex event patterns.

CEP focuses more on complexity, providing rich analytics. However, as a result, speed of execution may be adversely affected. In general, CEP is considered to be a superset of ESP and often the output of ESP results in the generation of synthetic events that can be fed into CEP.

Realtime Big Data Processing and SCV

While designing a realtime Big Data processing system, the SCV principle needs to be kept in mind. In light of this principle, consider a hard-realtime and a near-realtime Big Data processing system. For both hard-realtime and near-realtime scenarios, we assume that data loss is unacceptable; in other words, high data volume (V) processing is required for both the systems.

Note that the requirement that the data loss should not occur does not mean that all data will actually be processed in realtime. Rather, it means that the system captures all input data and that the data is always persisted to disk either directly by writing it to on-disk storage or indirectly to a disk serving as a persistence layer for in-memory storage.

In the case of a hard-realtime system, a fast response (S) is required, hence consistency (C) will be compromised if high volume data (V) needs to be processed in memory. This scenario will require the use of sampling or approximation techniques, which will in turn generate less accurate results but with tolerable precision in a timely manner.

In the case of a near-realtime system, a reasonably fast response (S) is required, hence consistency (C) can be guaranteed if high volume data (V) needs to be processed in memory. Results will be more accurate when compared to a hard-realtime system since the complete dataset can be used instead of taking samples or employing approximation techniques.

Thus, in the context of Big Data processing, a hard-realtime system requires a compromise on consistency (C) to guarantee a fast response (S) while a near-realtime system can compromise speed (S) to guarantee consistent results (C).

Realtime Big Data Processing and MapReduce

MapReduce is generally unsuitable for realtime Big Data processing. There are several reasons for this, not the least of which is the amount of overhead associated with MapReduce job creation and coordination. MapReduce is intended for the batch-oriented processing of large amounts of data that has been stored to disk. MapReduce cannot process data incrementally and can only process complete datasets. It therefore requires all input data to be available in its entirety before the execution of the data processing job. This is at odds with the requirements for realtime data processing as realtime processing involves data that is often incomplete and continuously arriving via a stream.

Additionally, with MapReduce a reduce task cannot generally start before the completion of all map tasks. First, the map output is persisted locally on each node that runs the map function. Next, the map output is copied over the network to the nodes that run the reduce function, introducing processing latency. Similarly, the results of one reducer cannot be directly fed into another reducer, rather the results would have to be passed to a mapper first in a subsequent MapReduce job.

As demonstrated, MapReduce is generally not useful for realtime processing, especially when hard-realtime constraints are present. There are however some strategies that can enable the use of MapReduce in near-realtime Big Data processing scenarios.

One strategy is to use in-memory storage to store data that serves as input to interactive queries that consist of MapReduce jobs. Alternatively, micro-batch MapReduce jobs can be deployed that are configured to run on comparatively smaller datasets at frequent intervals, such as every fifteen minutes. Another approach is to continuously run MapReduce jobs against on-disk datasets to create materialized views that can then be combined with small volume analysis results, obtained from newly arriving in-memory streaming data, for interactive query processing.

Given the predominance of smart devices and corporate desires to engage customers more proactively, advancements in realtime Big Data processing capabilities are occurring very quickly. Several open source Apache projects, specifically Spark, Storm and Tez, provide true realtime Big Data processing capabilities and are the foundation of a new generation of realtime processing solutions.

www.ingramcontent.com/pod-product-compliance
Lightning Source LLC
Chambersburg PA
CBHW072141170526
45158CB00004BA/1455